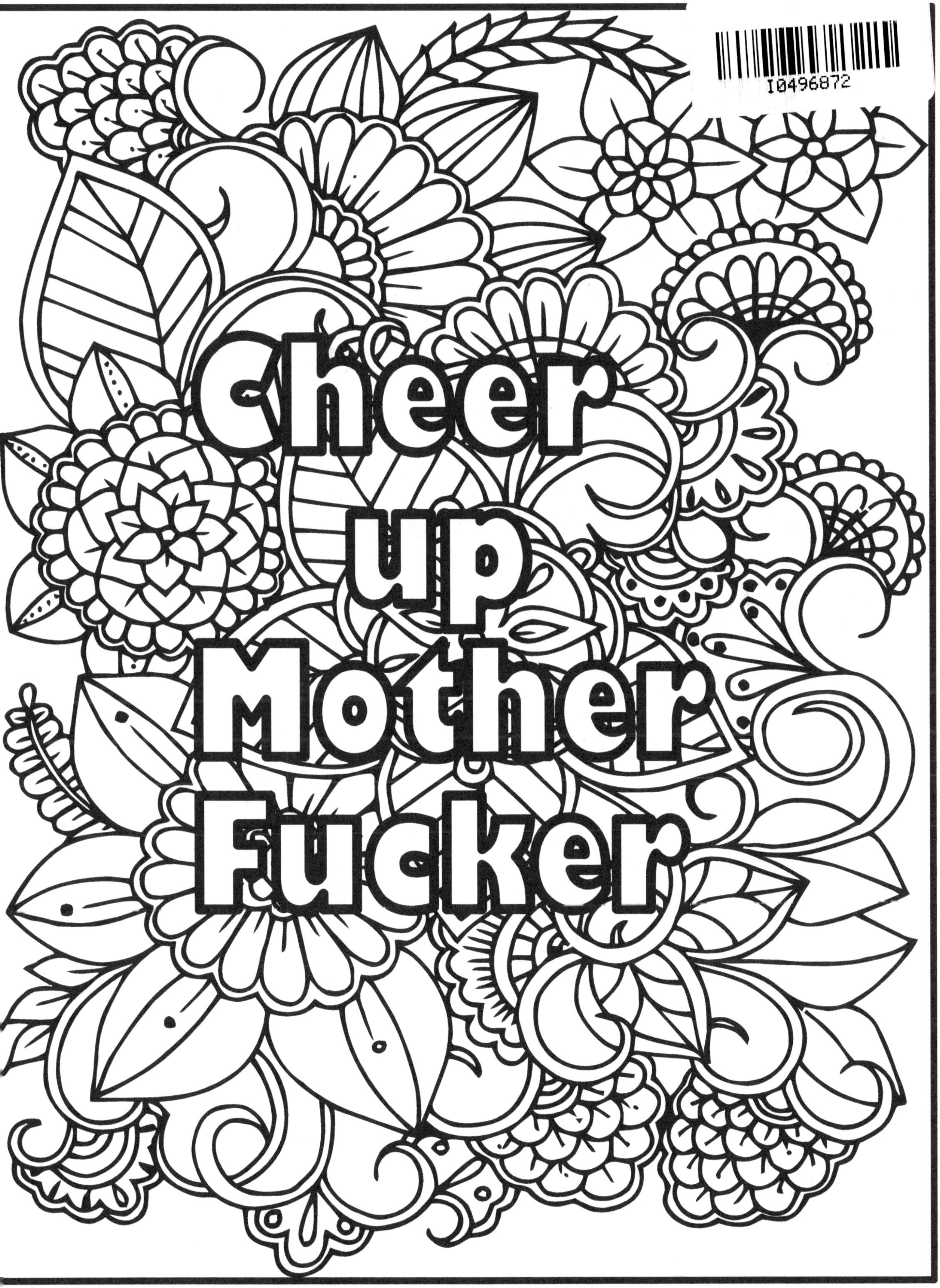
Cheer
up
Mother
Fucker

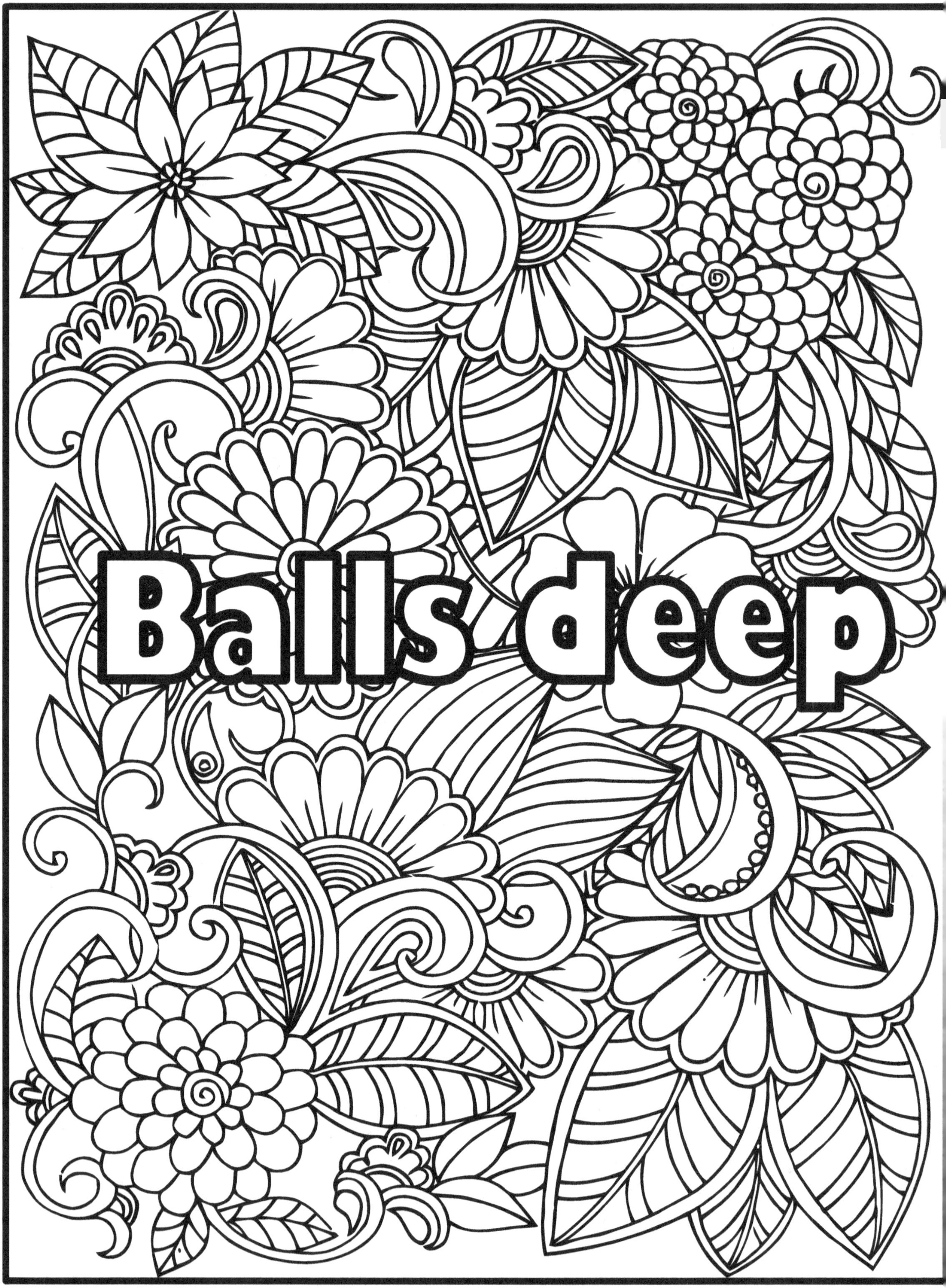
Balls deep

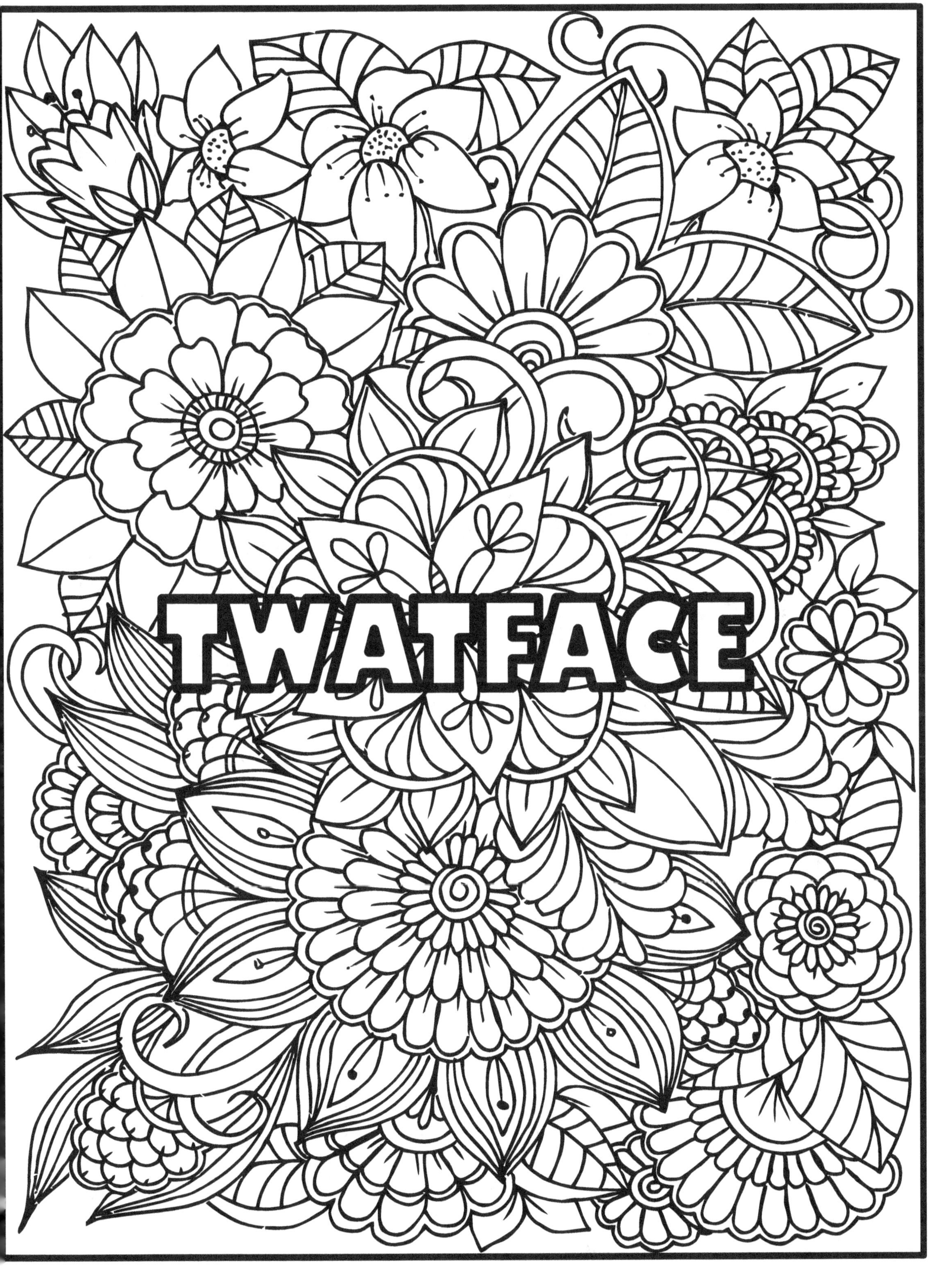
TWATFACE

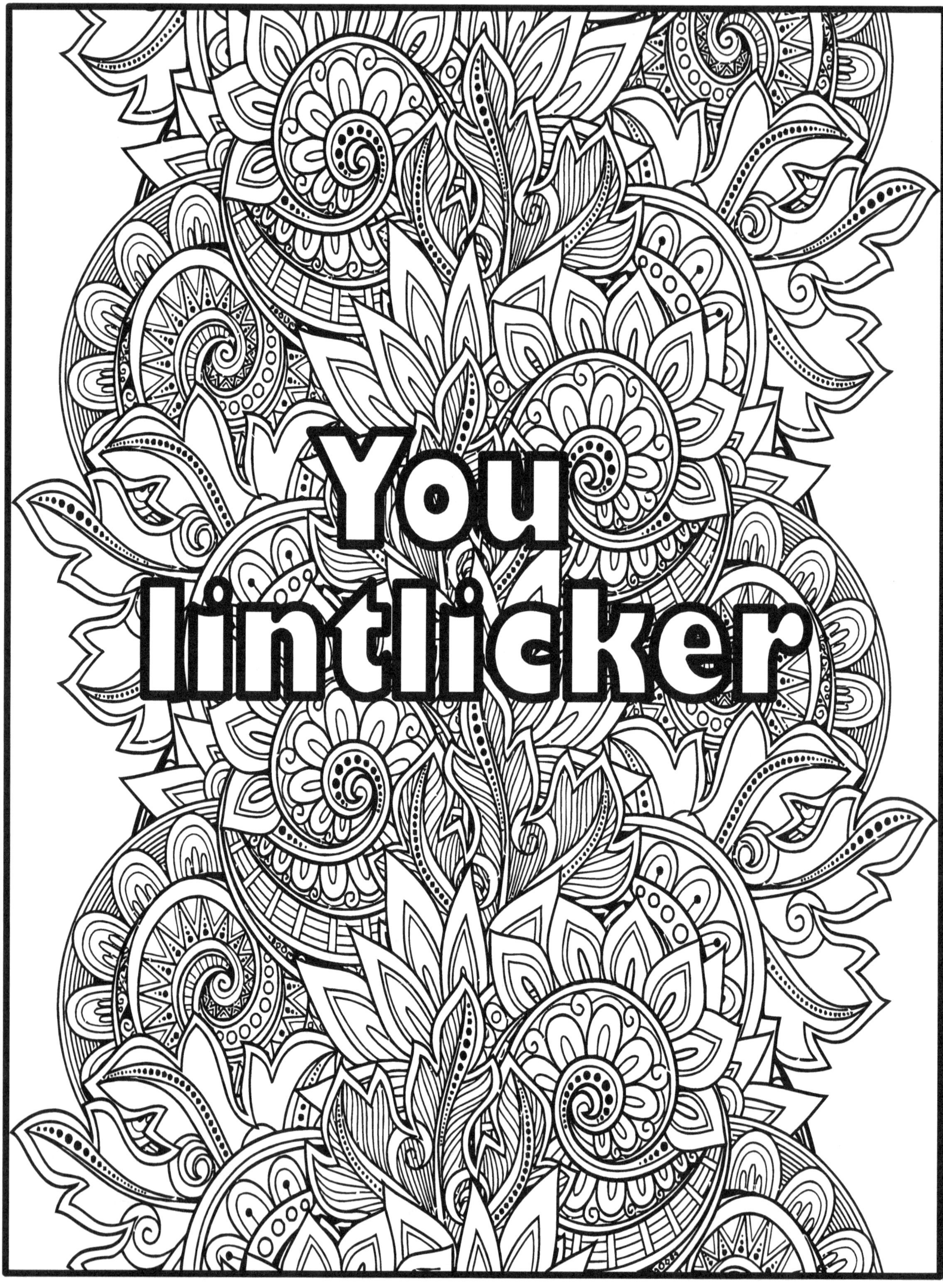
You
lintlicker

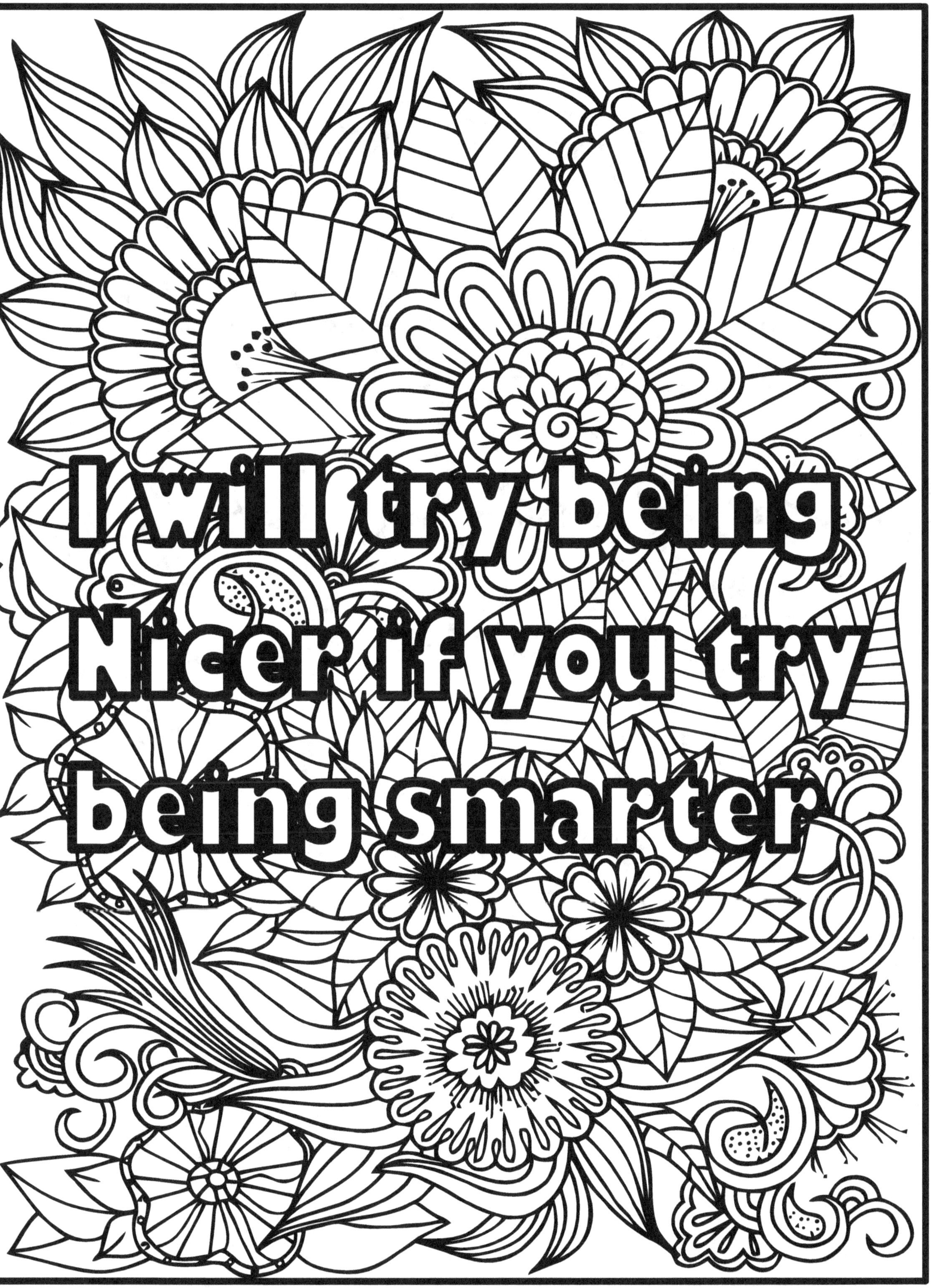
I will try being
Nicer if you try
being smarter

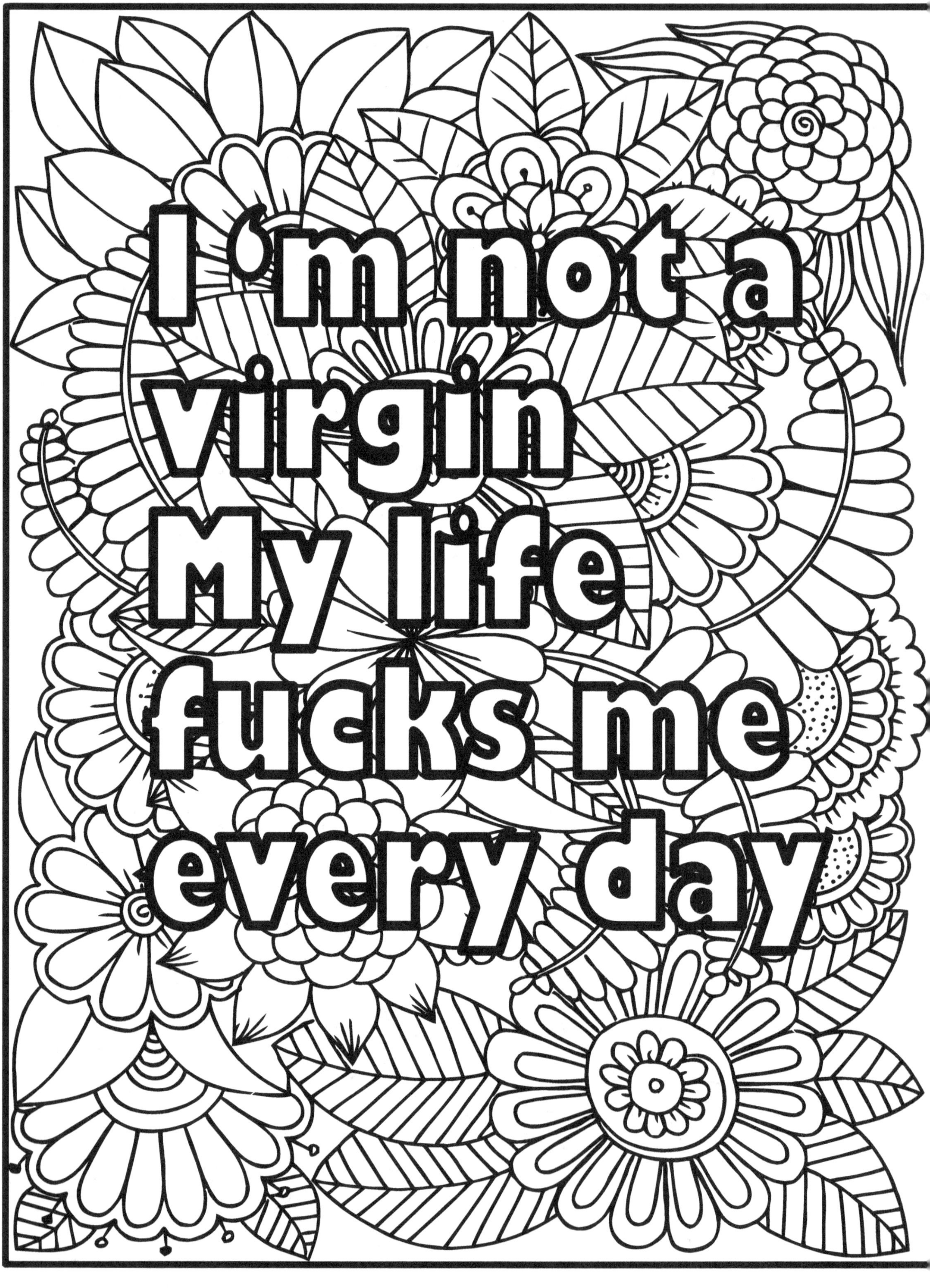
I'm not a
virgin
My life
fucks me
every day

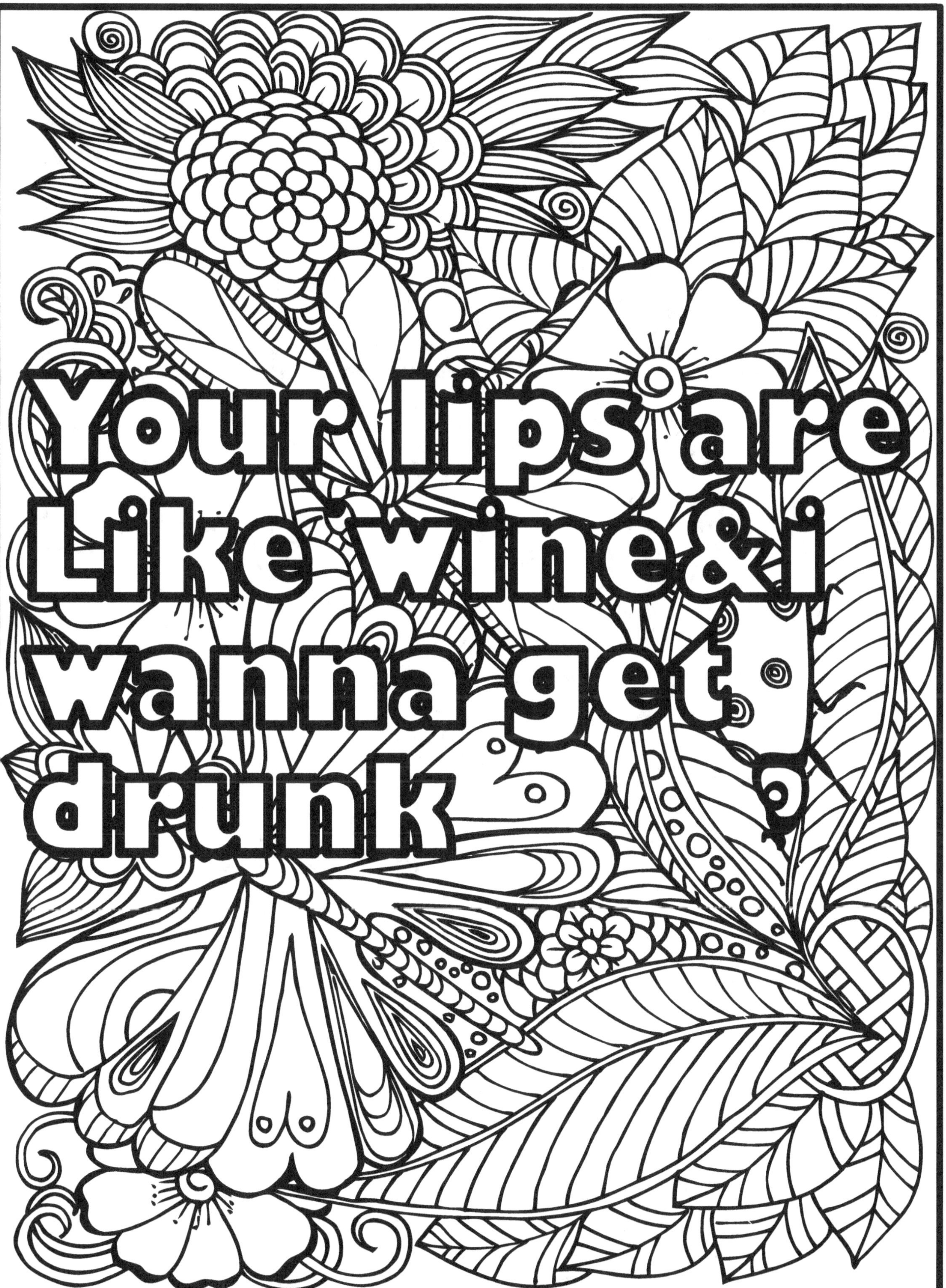
Your lips are
Like wine&i
wanna get
drunk

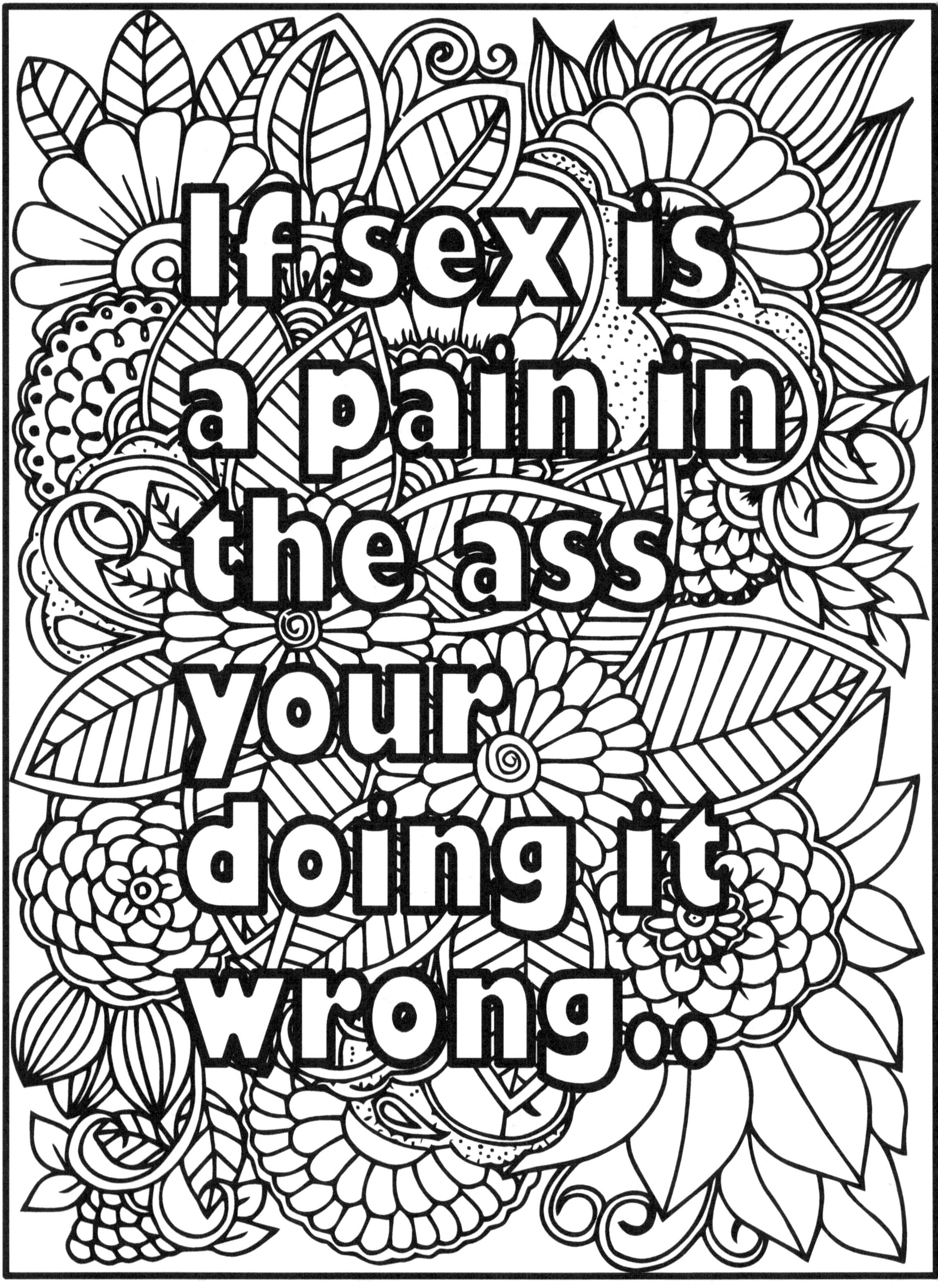
If sex is
a pain in
the ass
your
doing it
wrong...

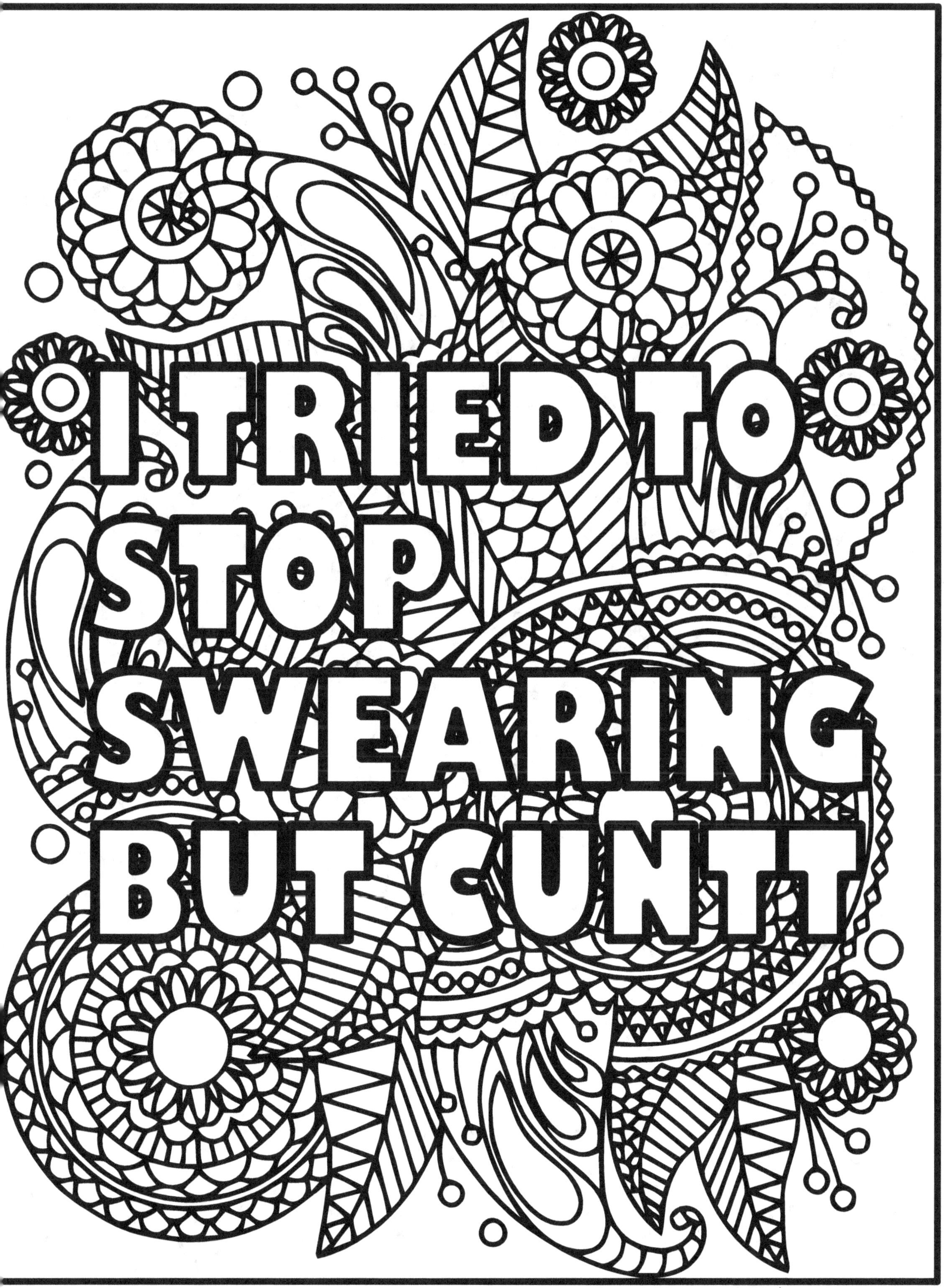
I TRIED TO
STOP
SWEARING
BUT CUNTT

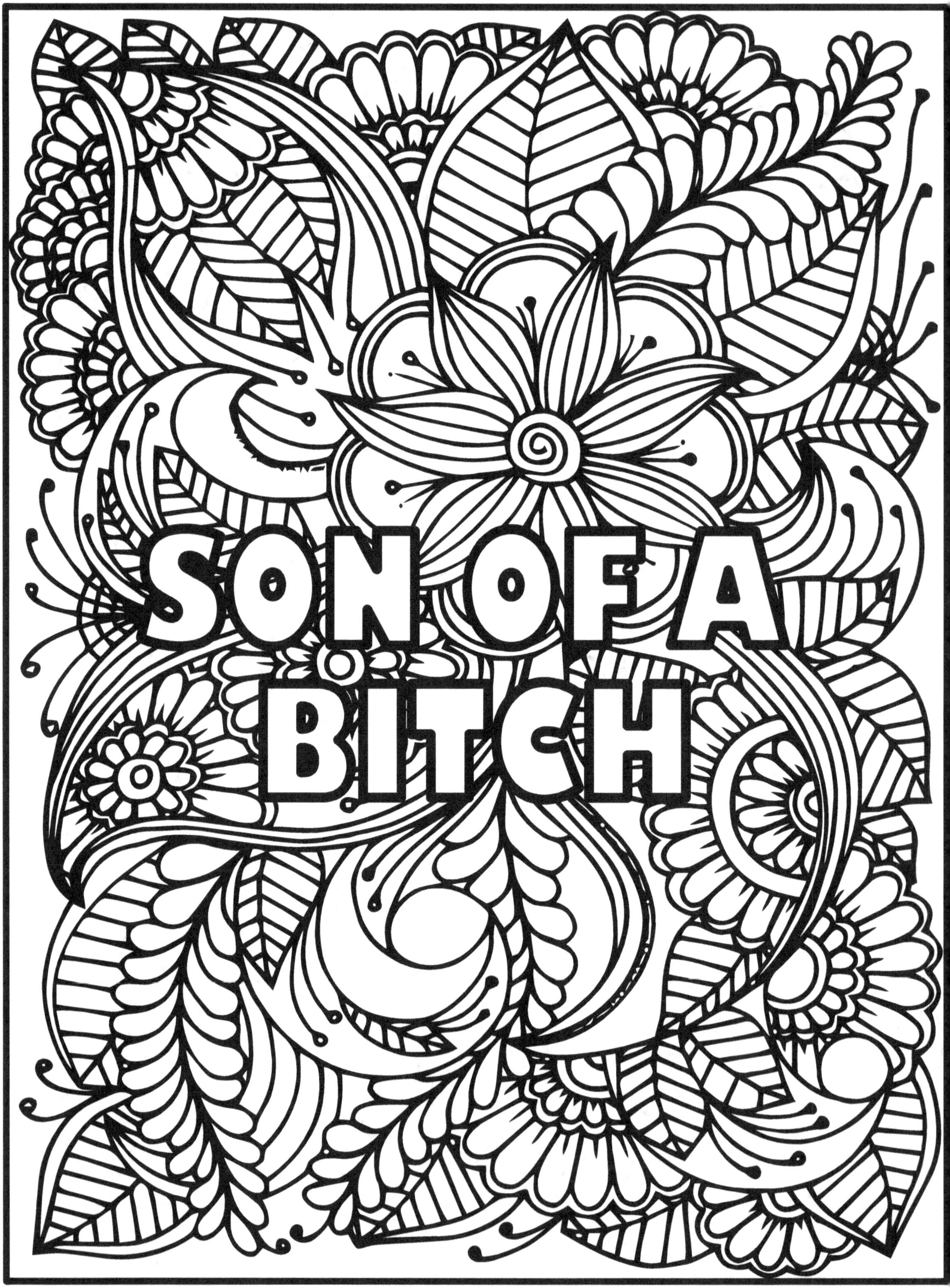
SON OF A
BITCH

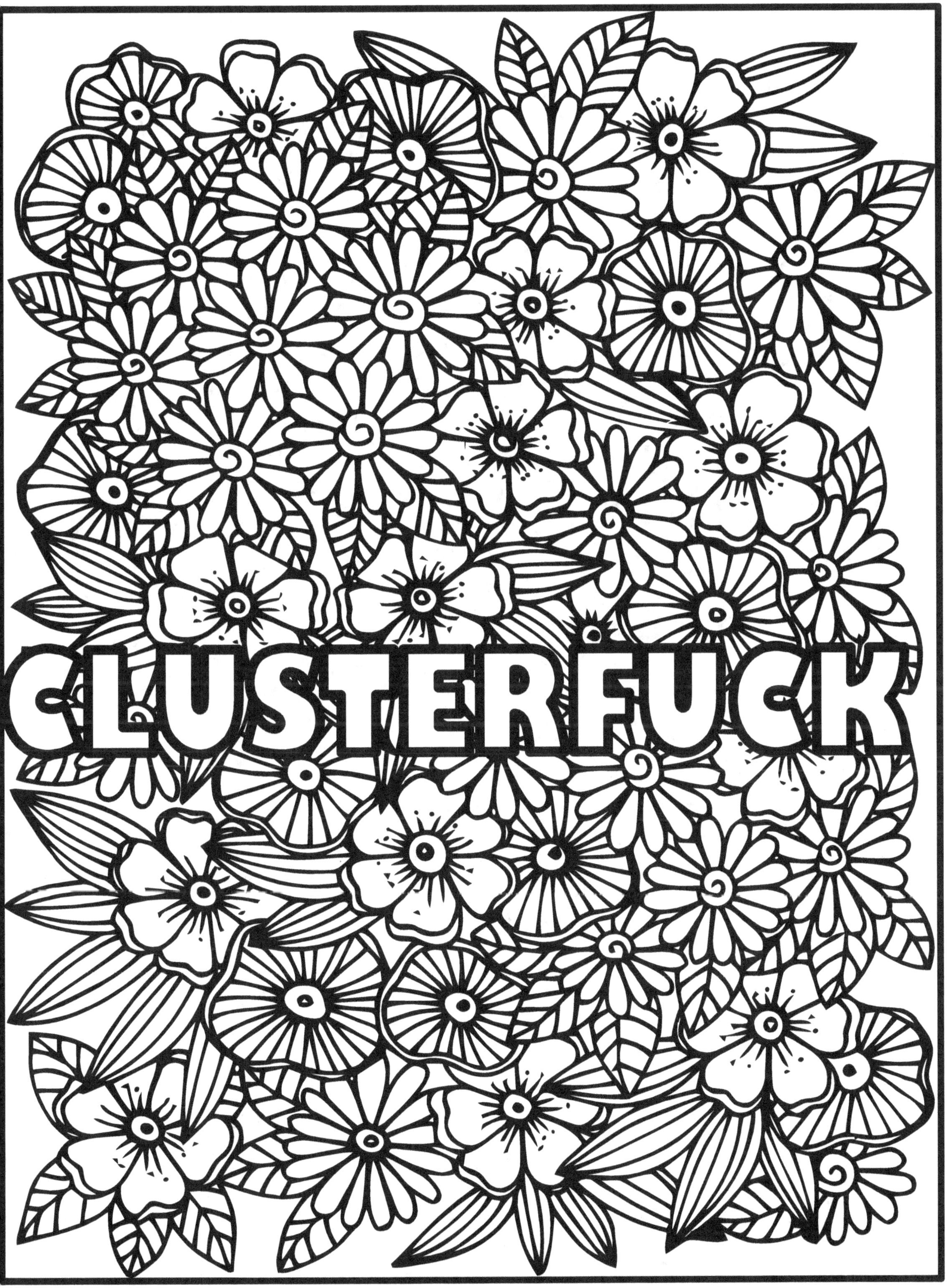
CLUSTERFUCK

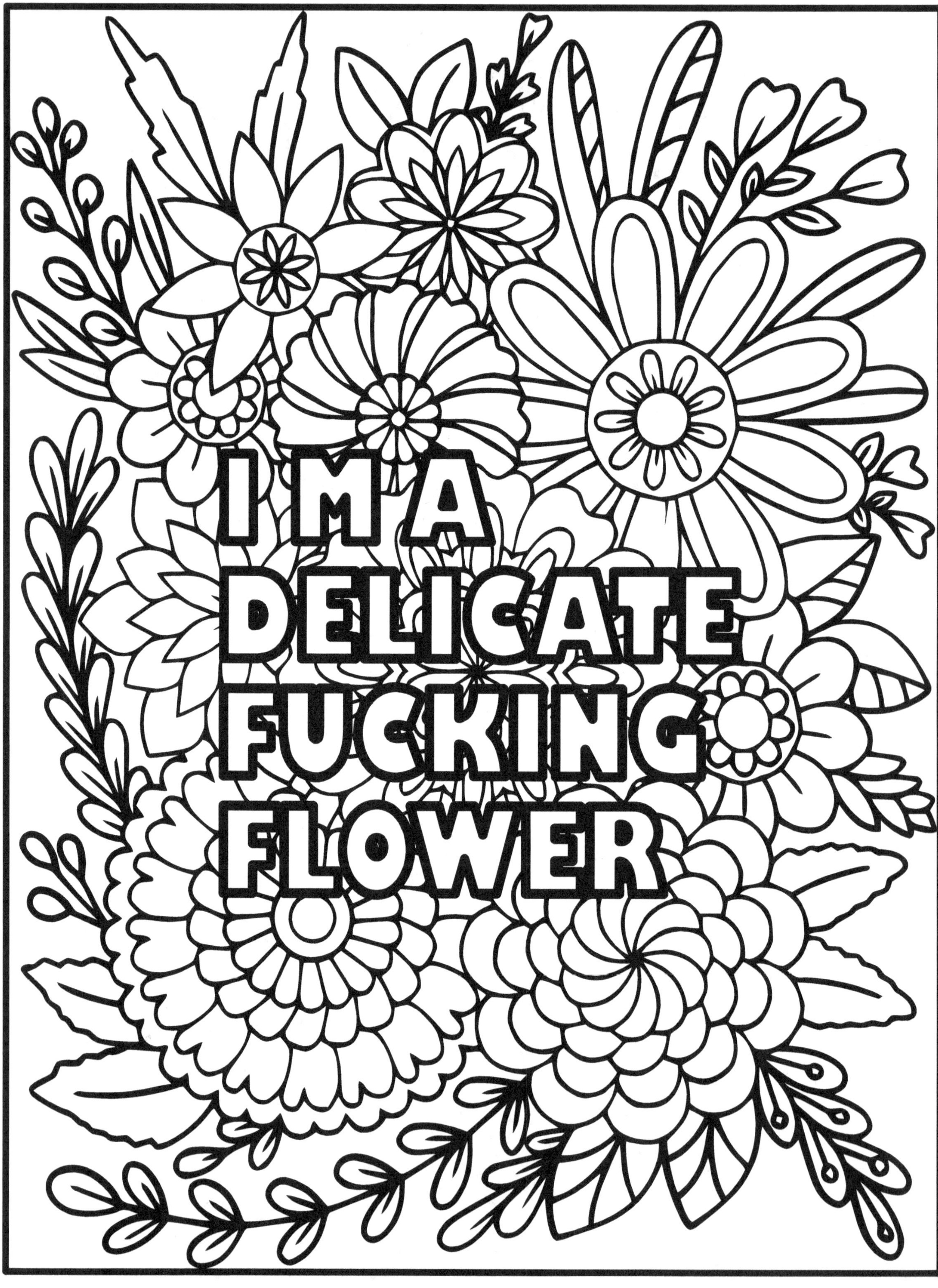
I M A
DELICATE
FUCKING
FLOWER

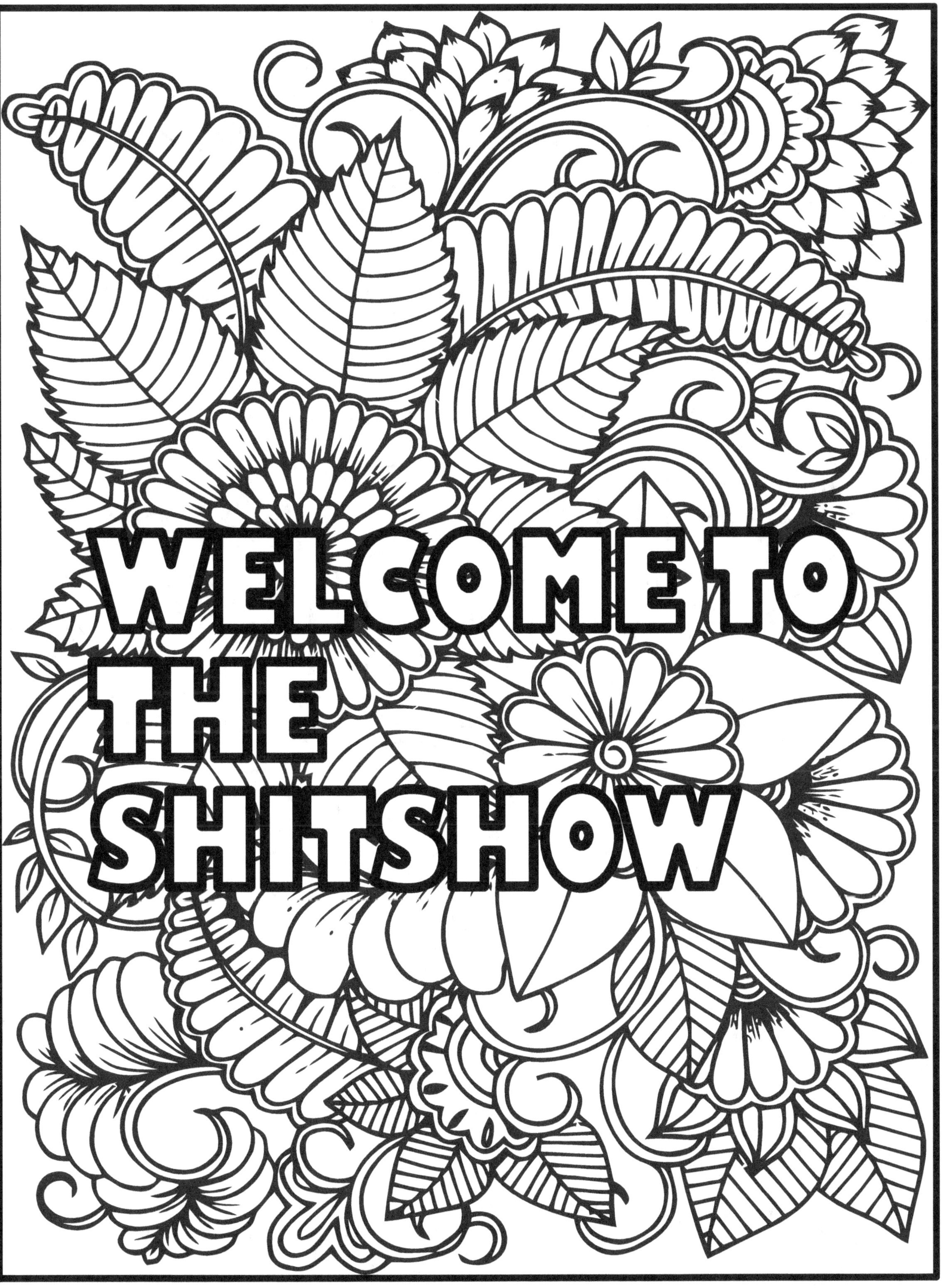
WELCOME TO
THE
SHITSHOW

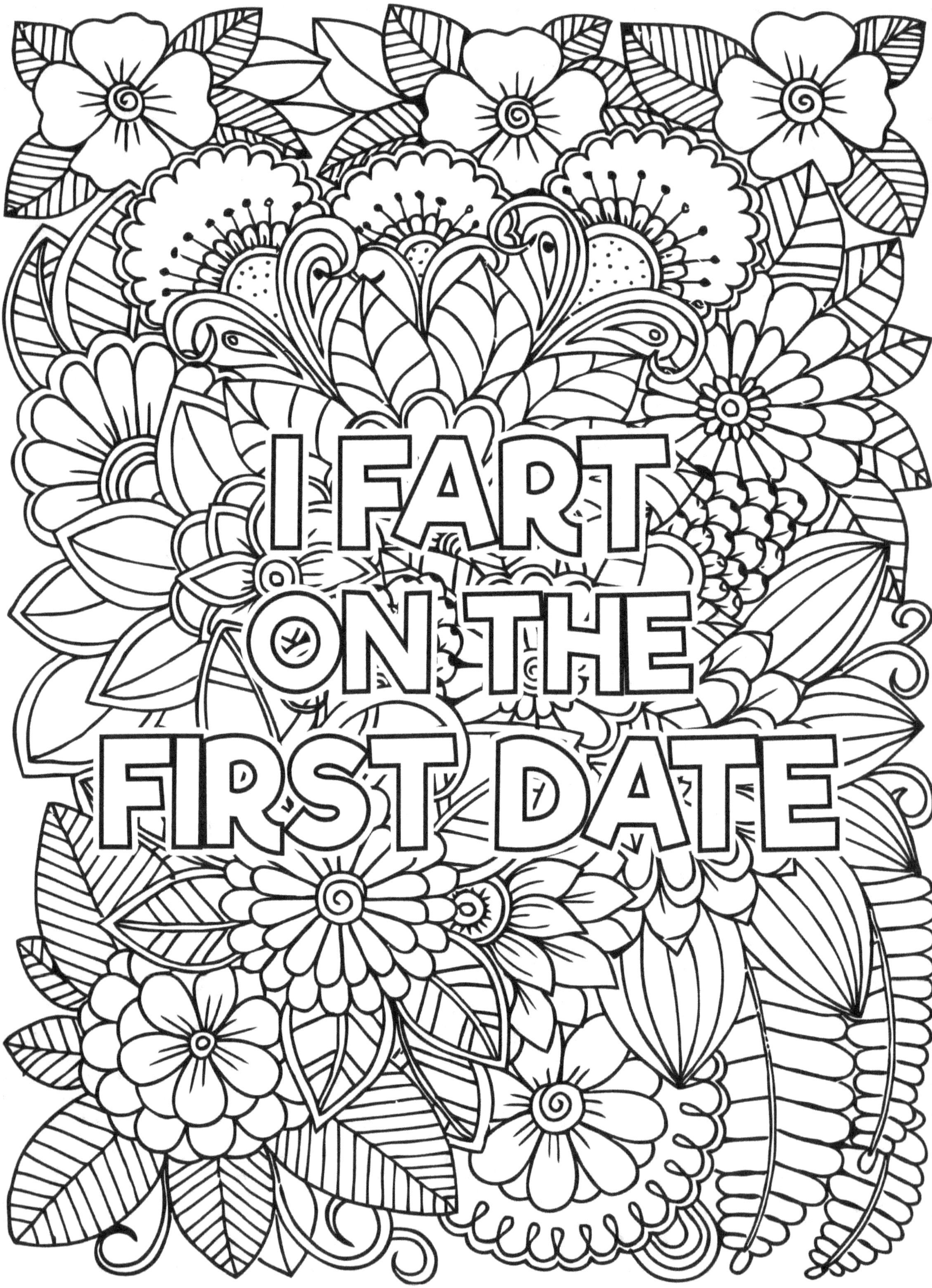
I FART
ON THE
FIRST DATE

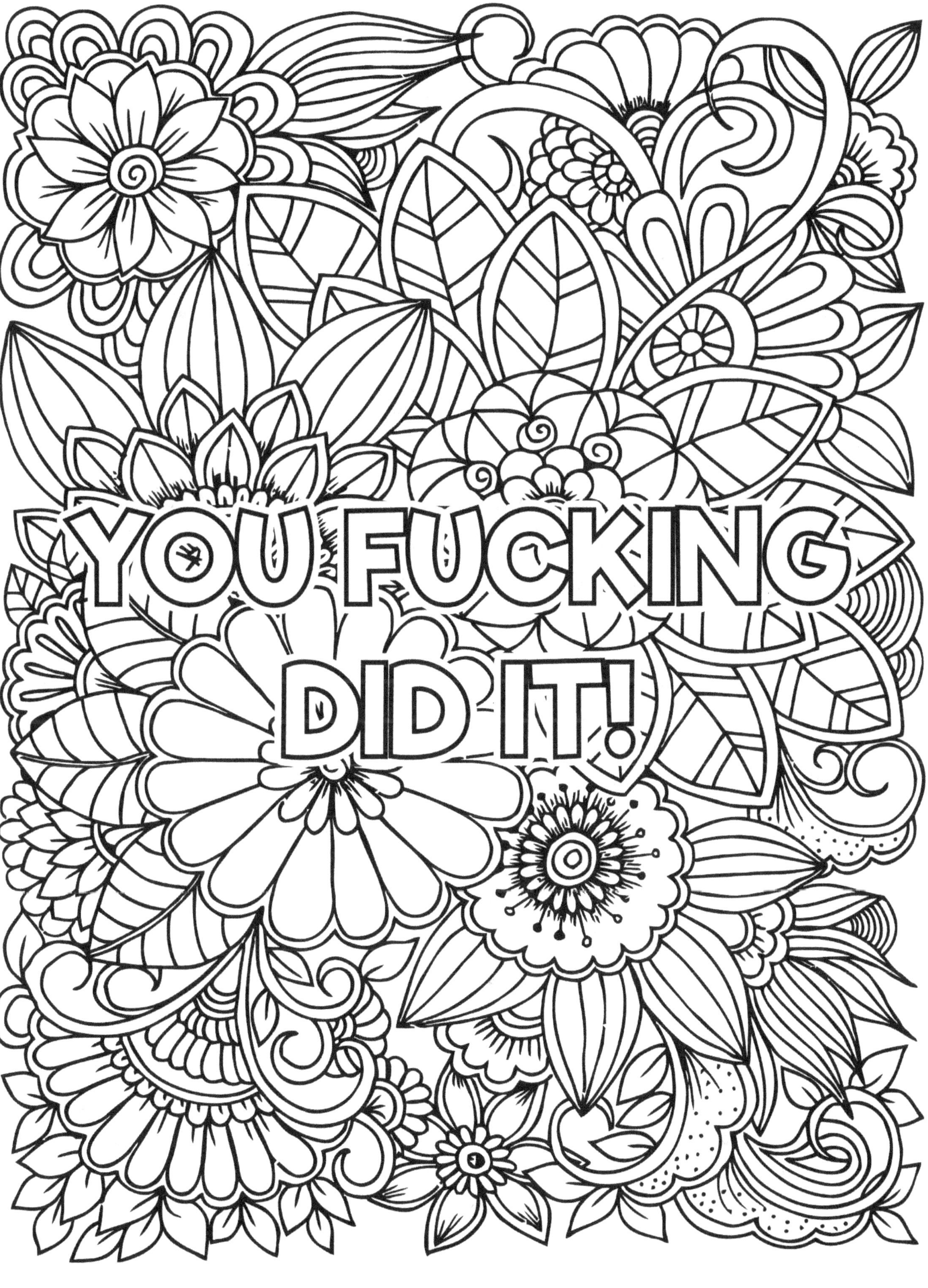
YOU FUCKING
DID IT!

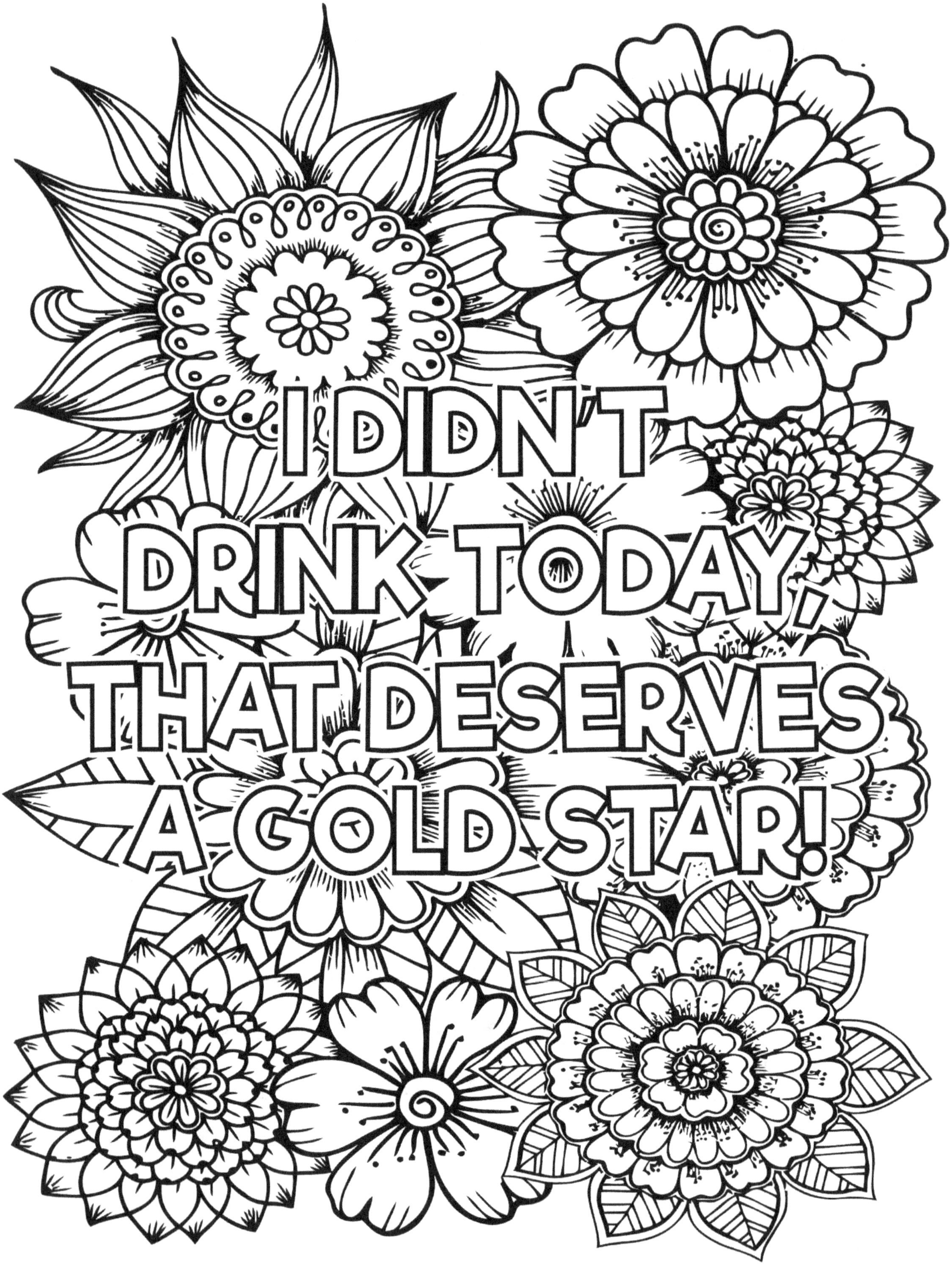
I DIDN'T
DRINK TODAY,
THAT DESERVES
A GOLD STAR!

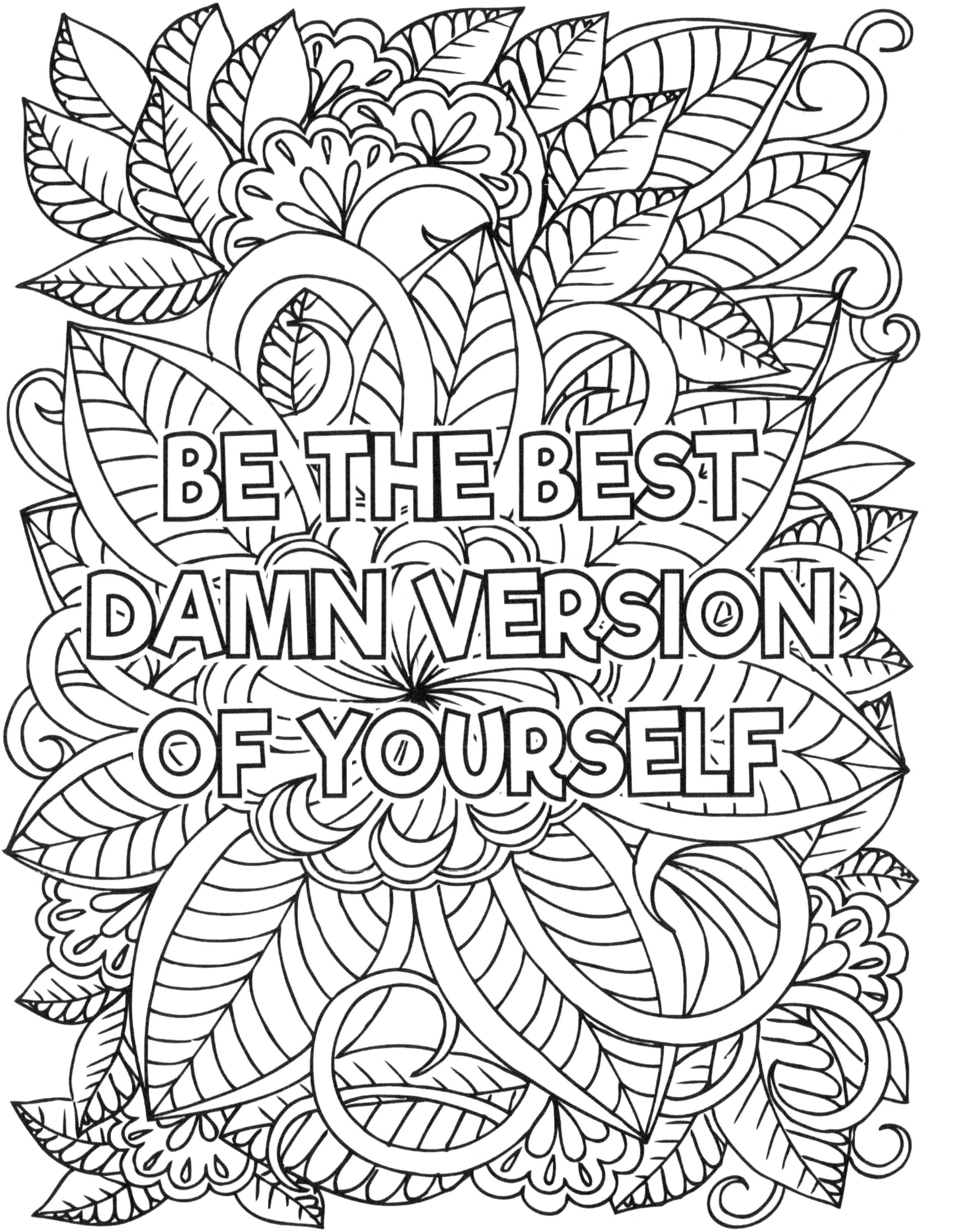
BE THE BEST
DAMN VERSION
OF YOURSELF

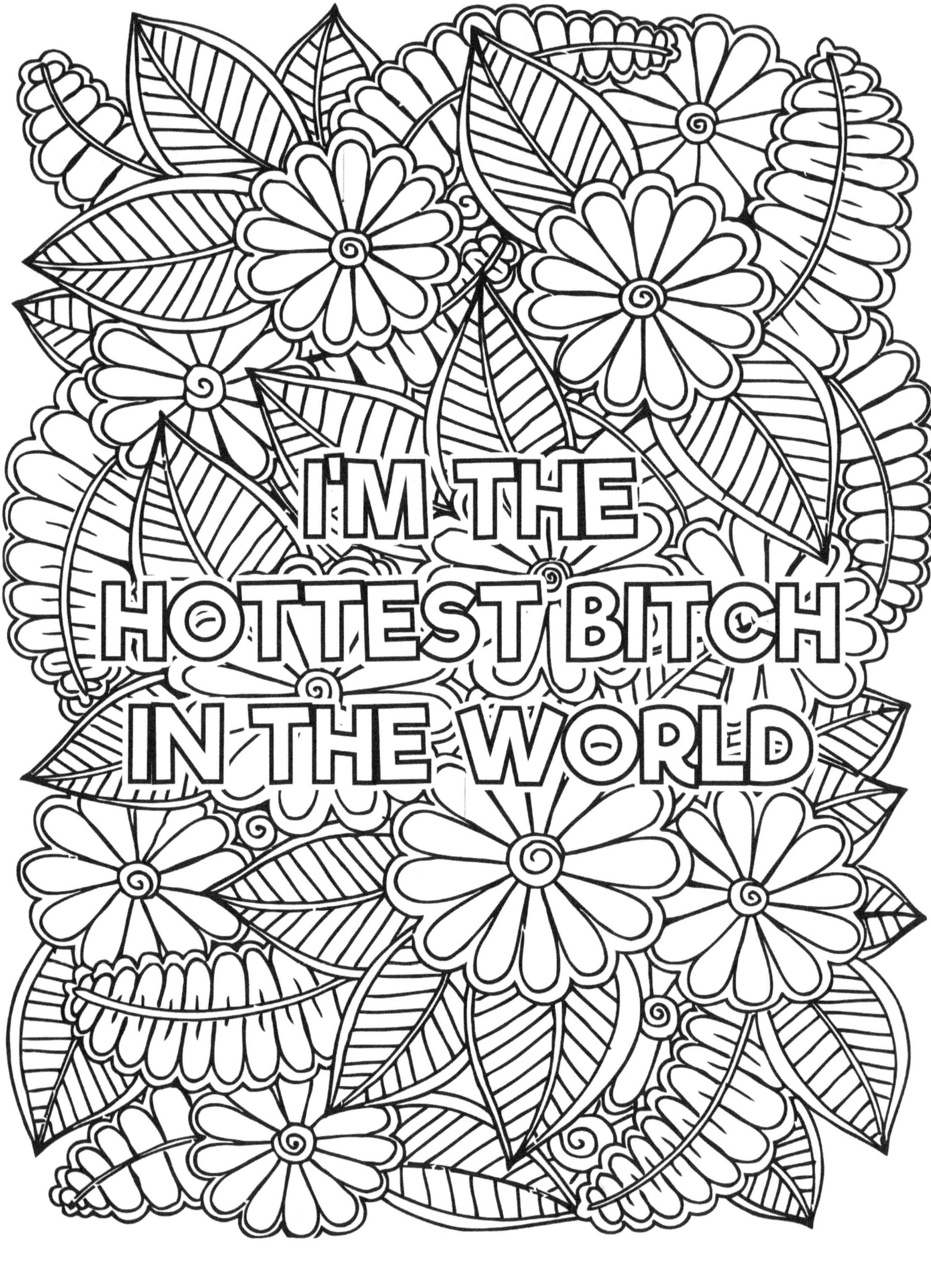
I'M THE
HOTTEST BITCH
IN THE WORLD

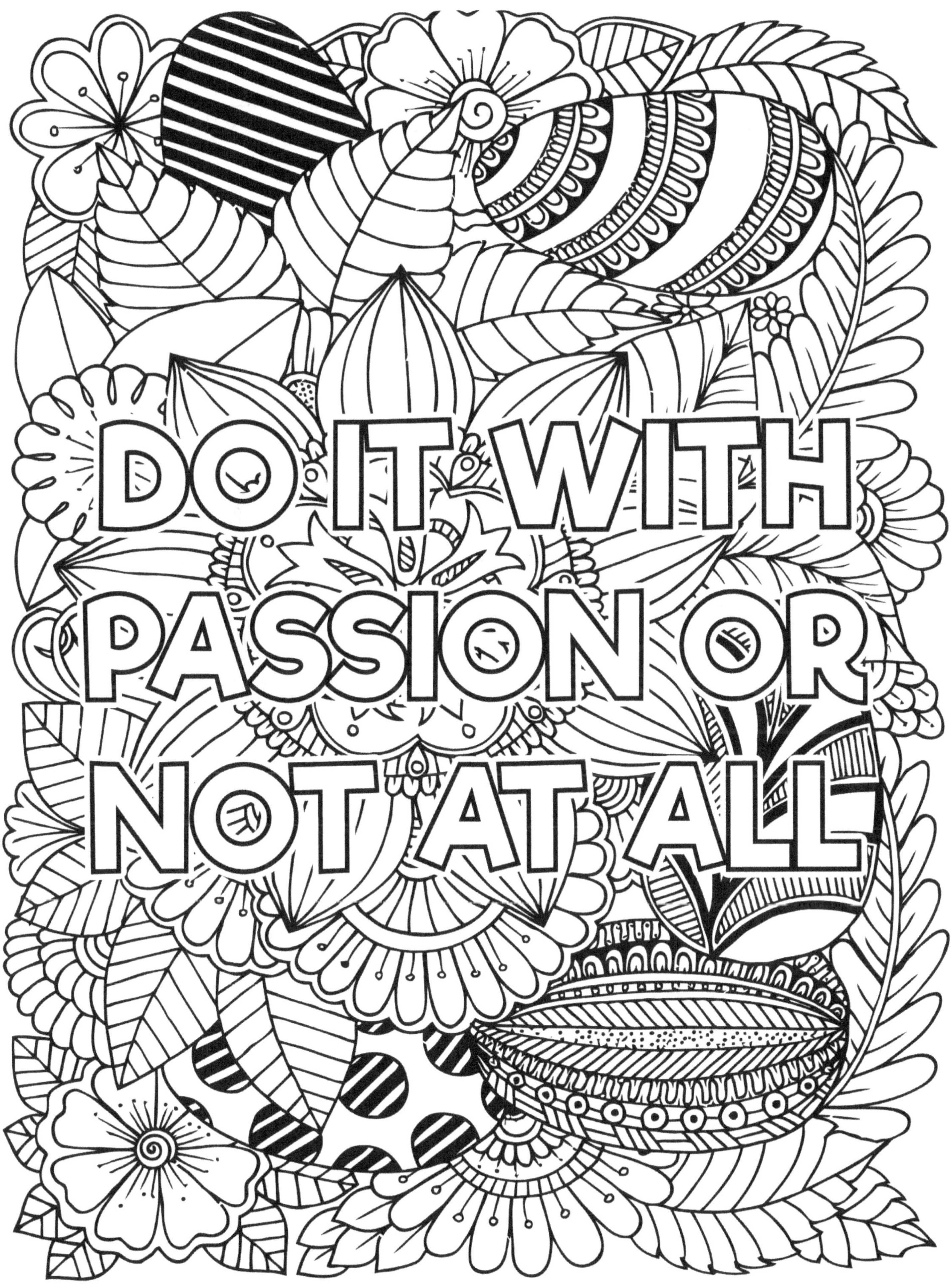
DO IT WITH
PASSION OR
NOT AT ALL

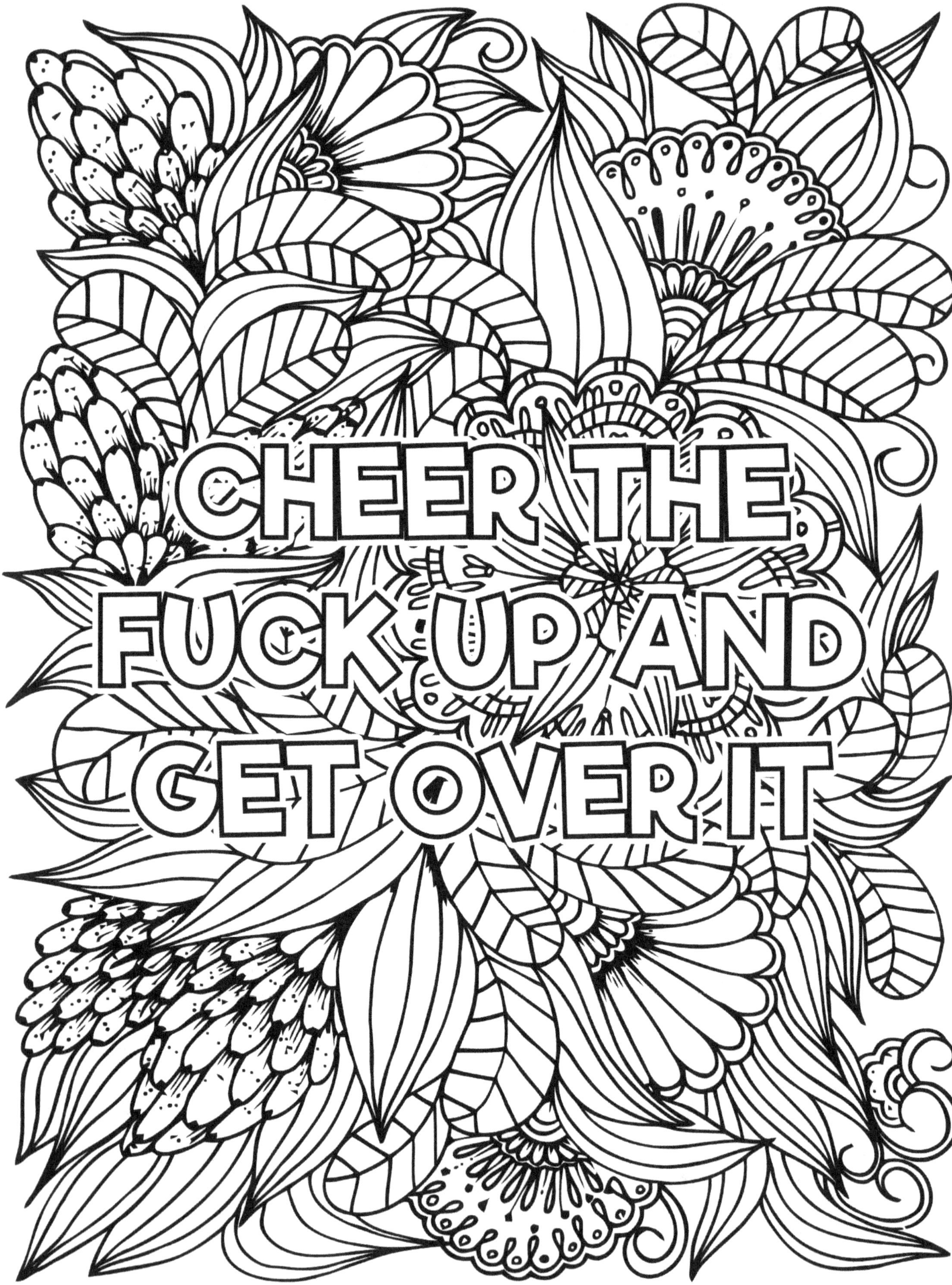
CHEER THE
FUCK UP AND
GET OVER IT

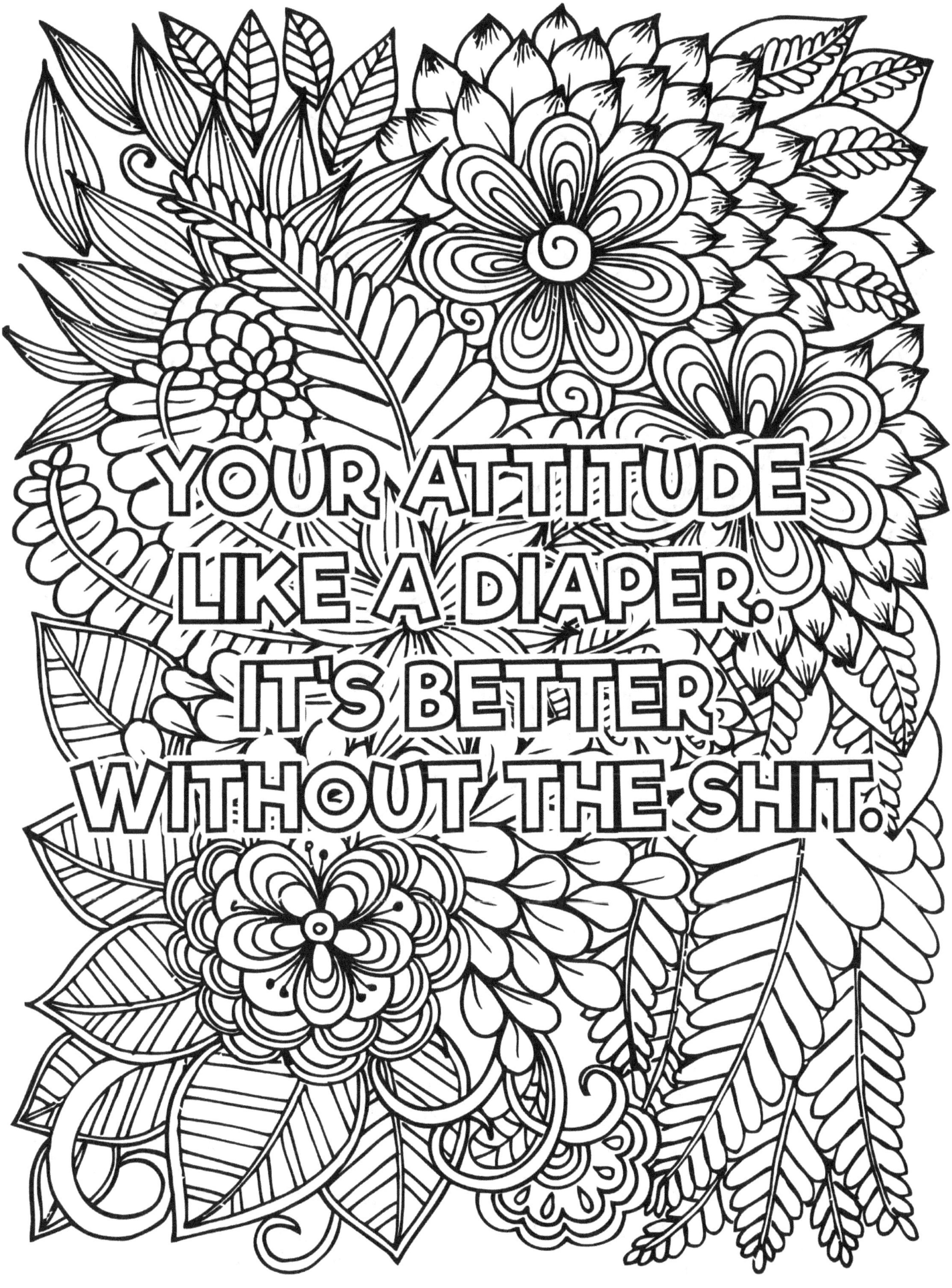
YOUR ATTITUDE
LIKE A DIAPER.
IT'S BETTER
WITHOUT THE SHIT.

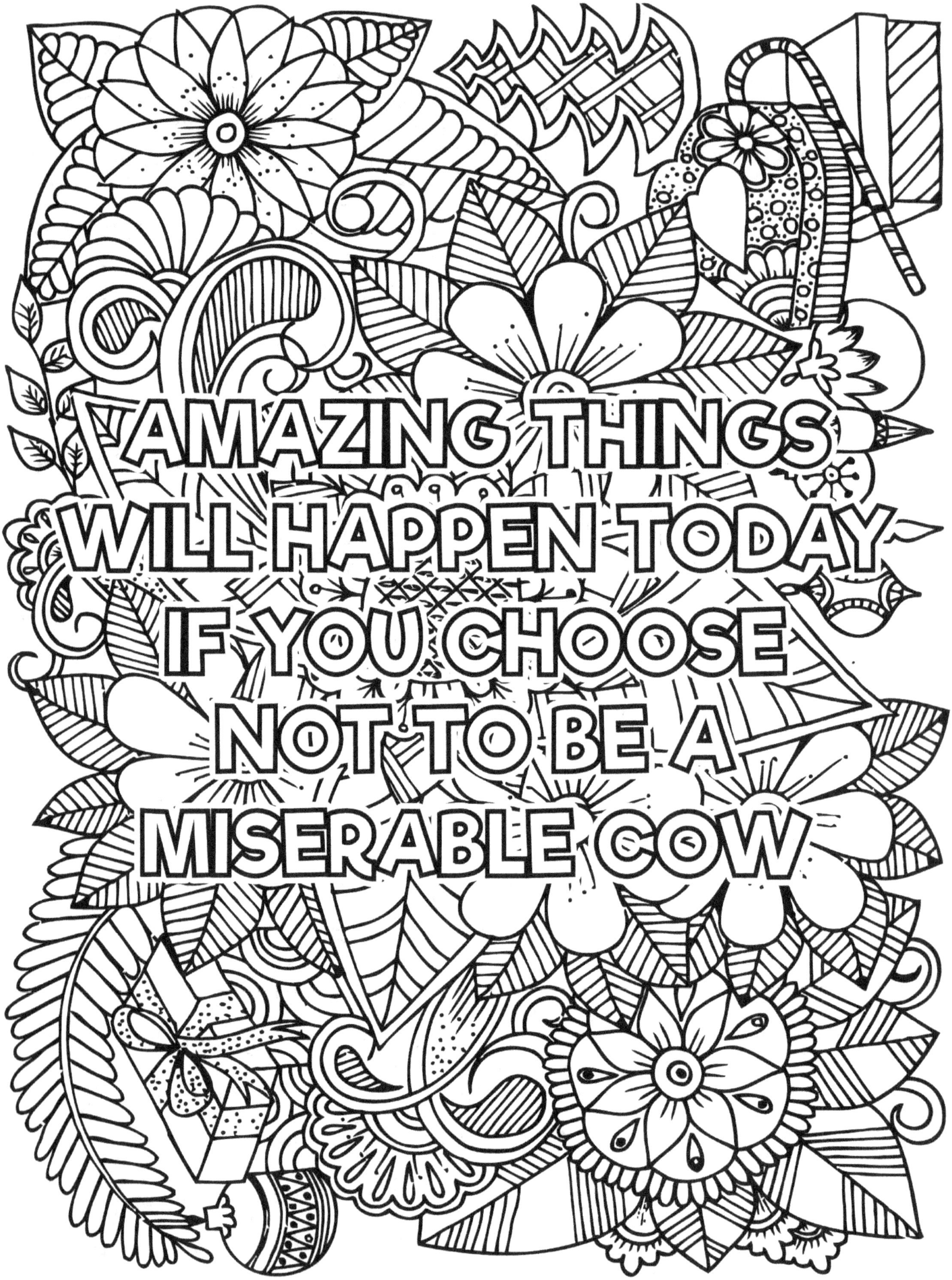
AMAZING THINGS
WILL HAPPEN TODAY
IF YOU CHOOSE
NOT TO BE A
MISERABLE COW

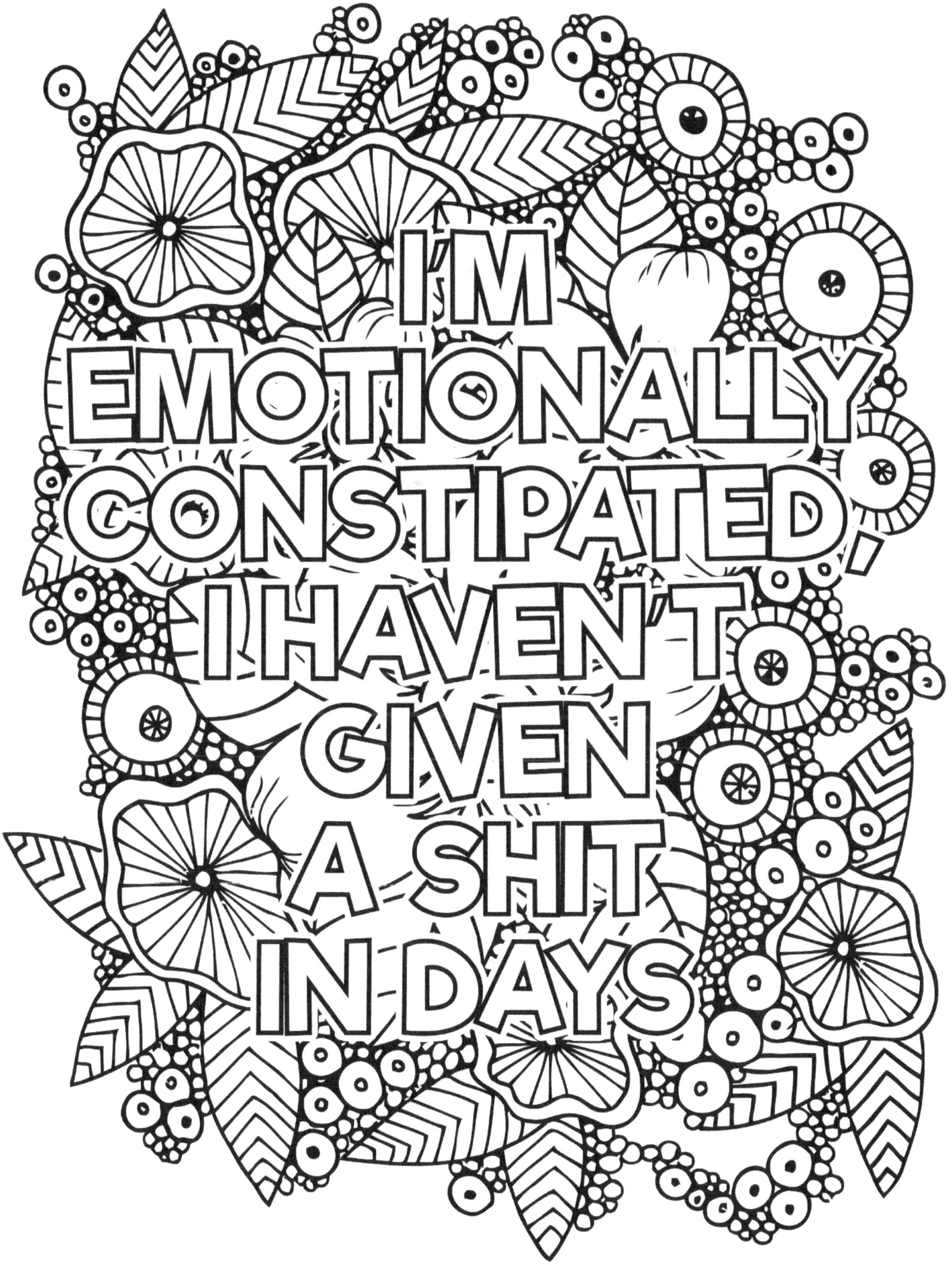
I'M EMOTIONALLY CONSTIPATED, I HAVEN'T GIVEN A SHIT IN DAYS

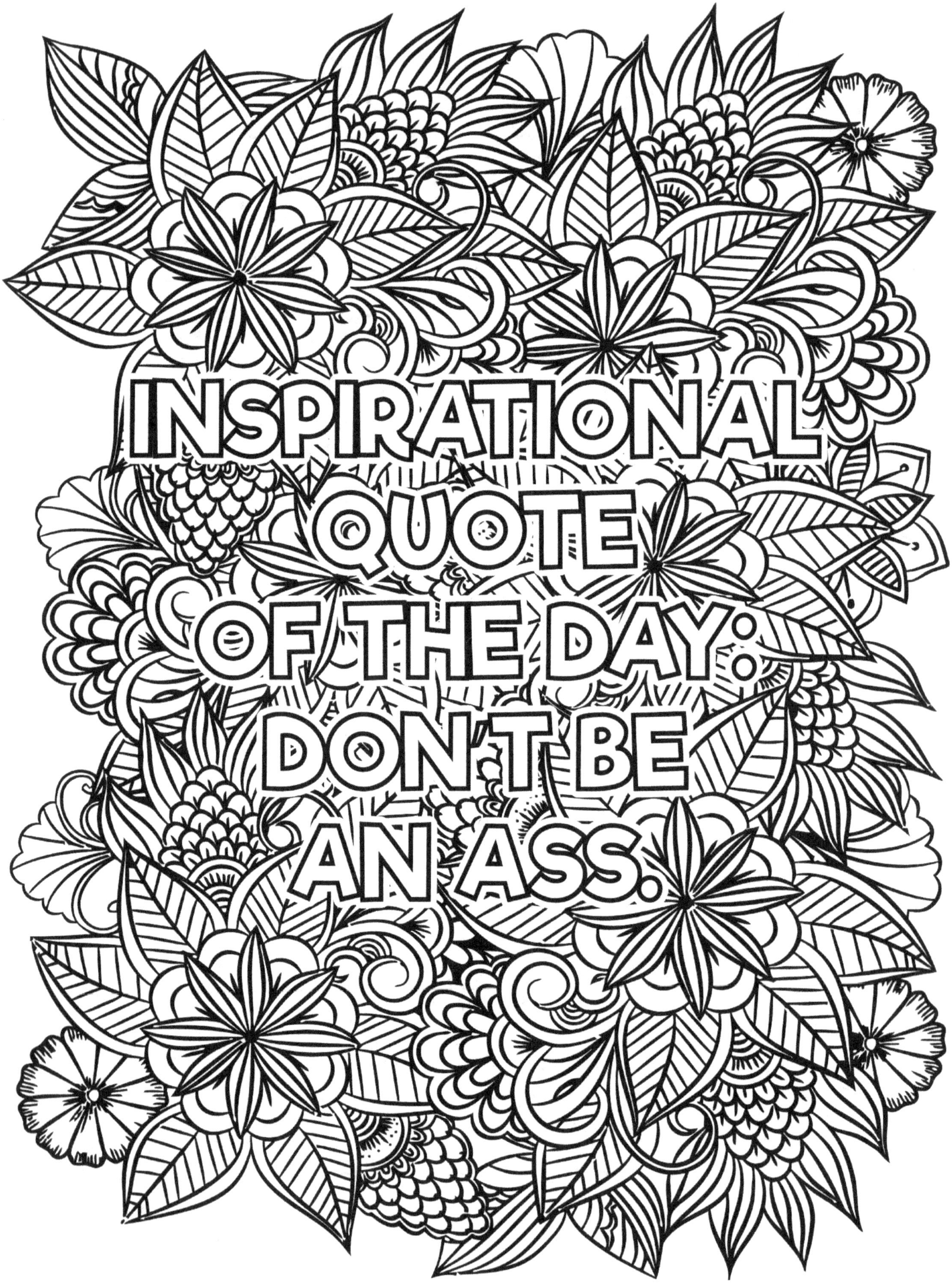
INSPIRATIONAL
QUOTE
OF THE DAY:
DON'T BE
AN ASS.

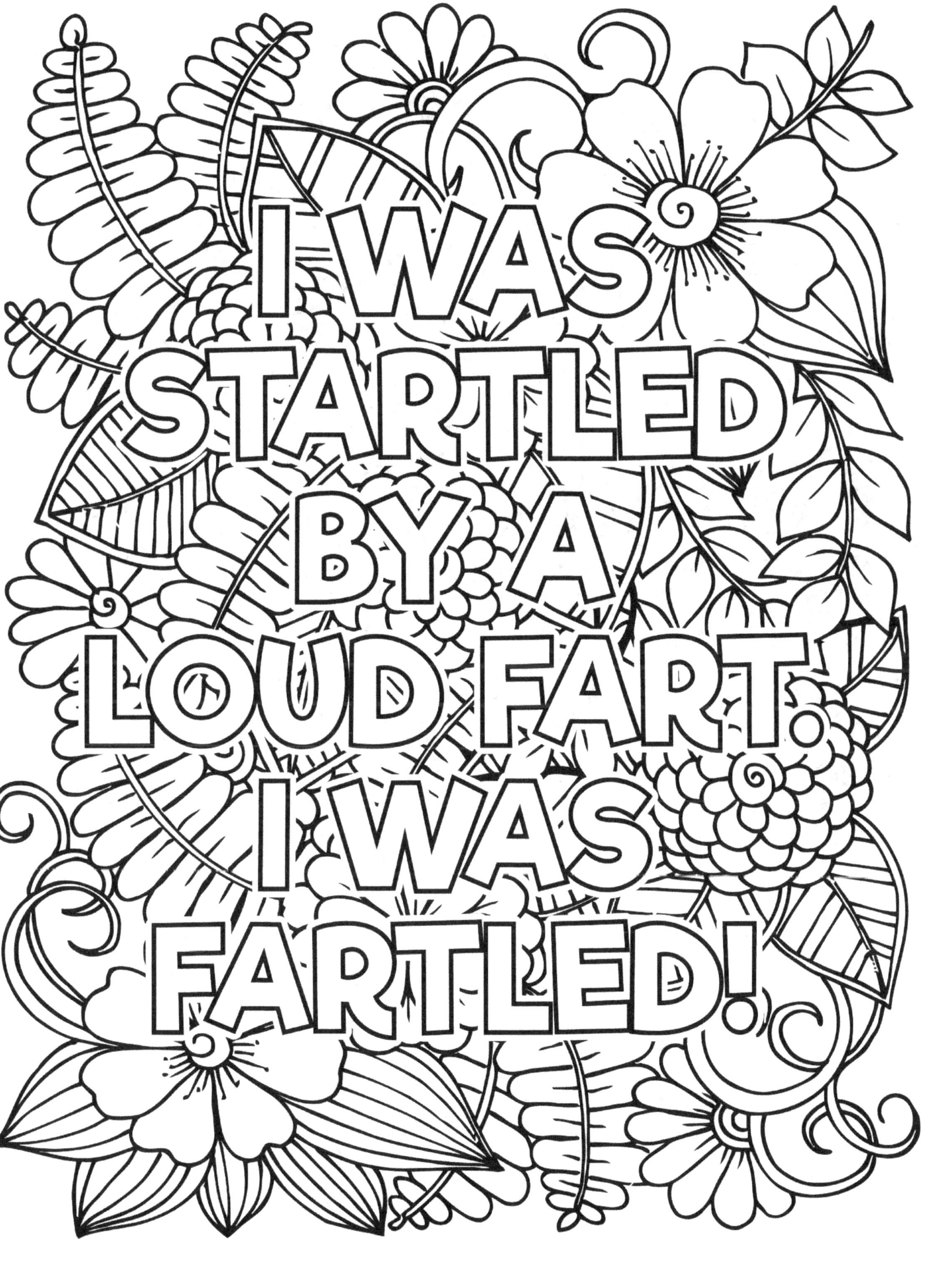
I WAS
STARTLED
BY A
LOUD FART.
I WAS
FARTLED!

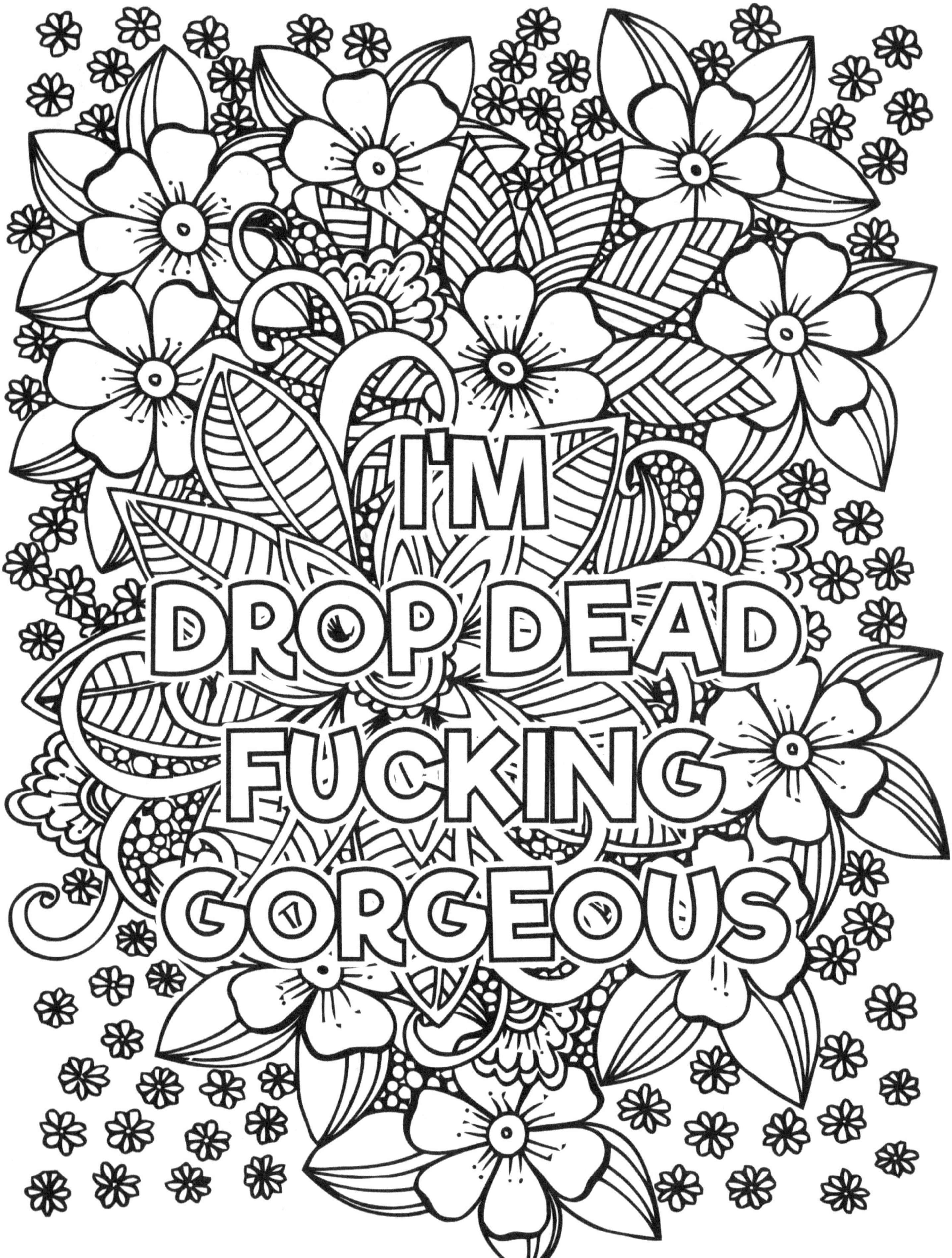
I'M
DROP DEAD
FUCKING
GORGEOUS

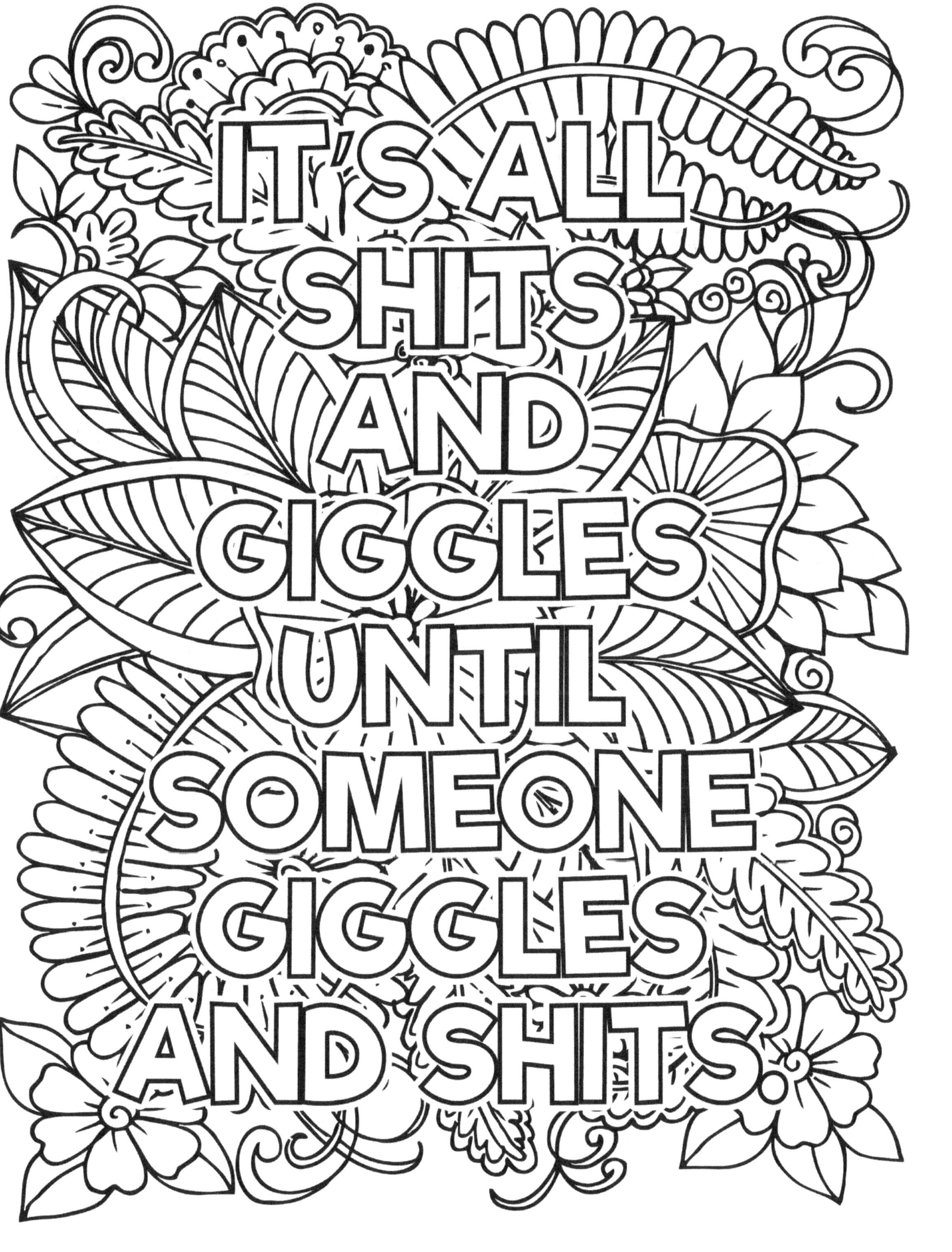
IT'S ALL
SHITS
AND
GIGGLES
UNTIL
SOMEONE
GIGGLES
AND SHITS.

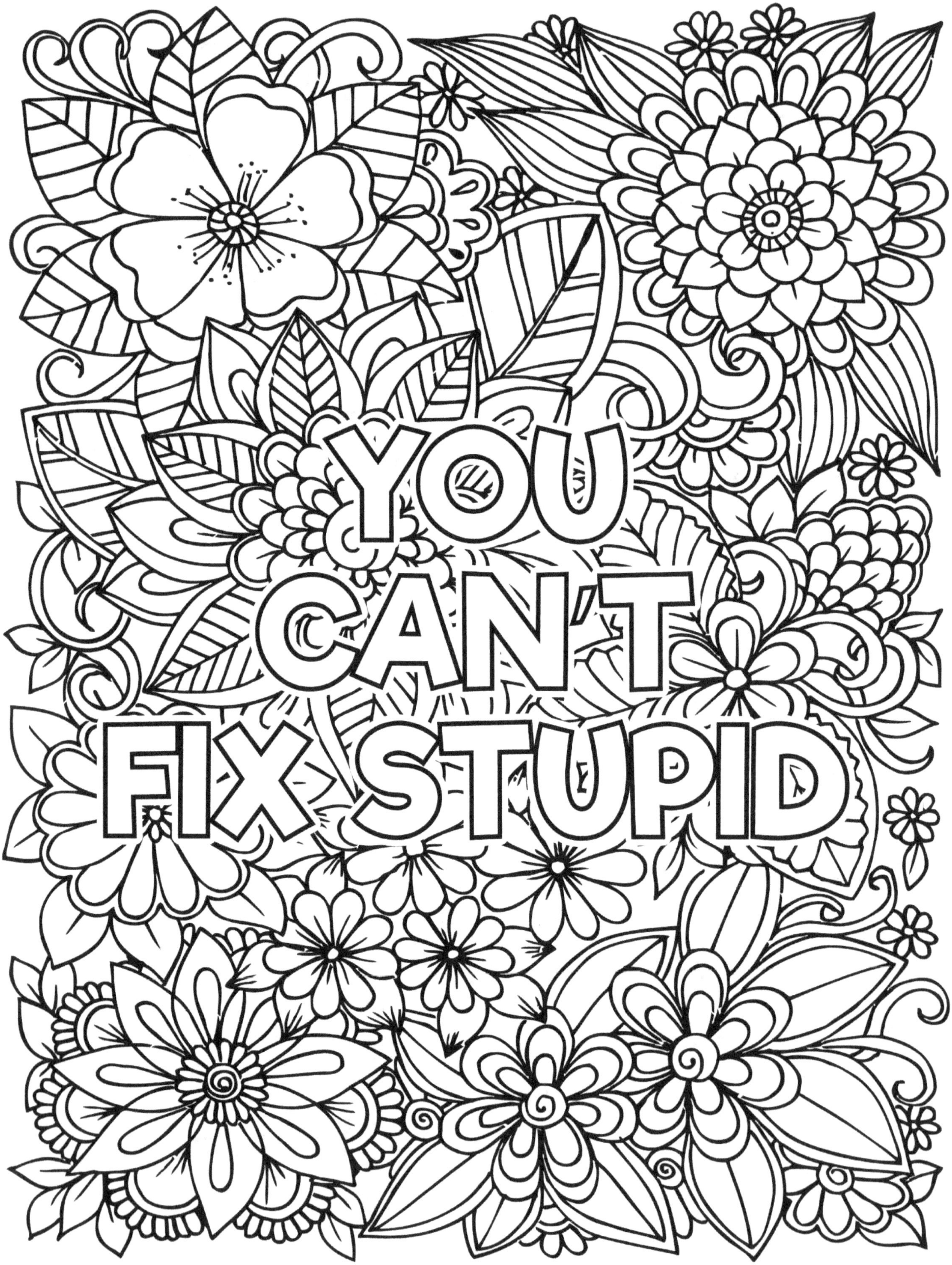
YOU
CAN'T
FIX STUPID

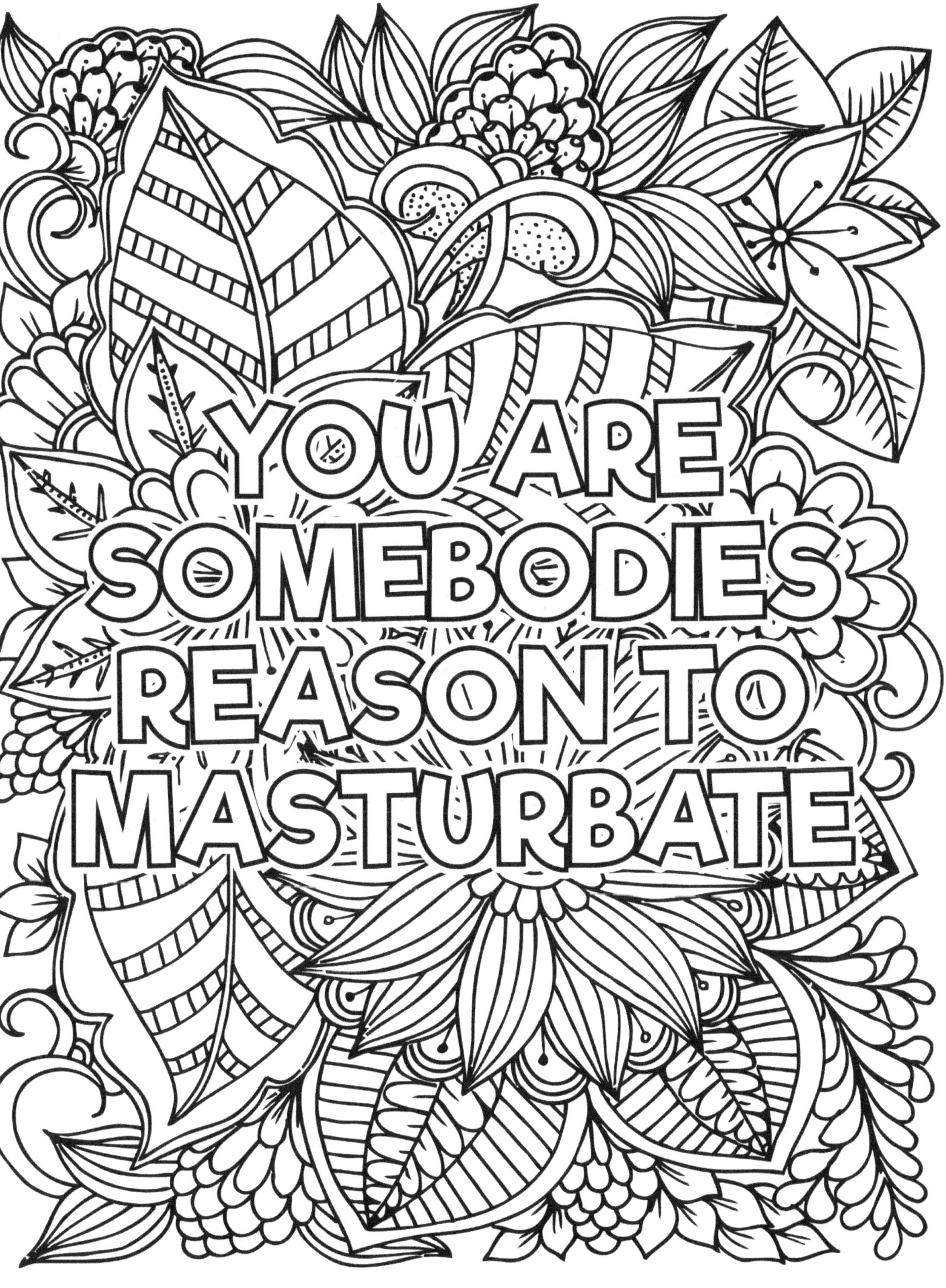
YOU ARE
SOMEBODIES
REASON TO
MASTURBATE

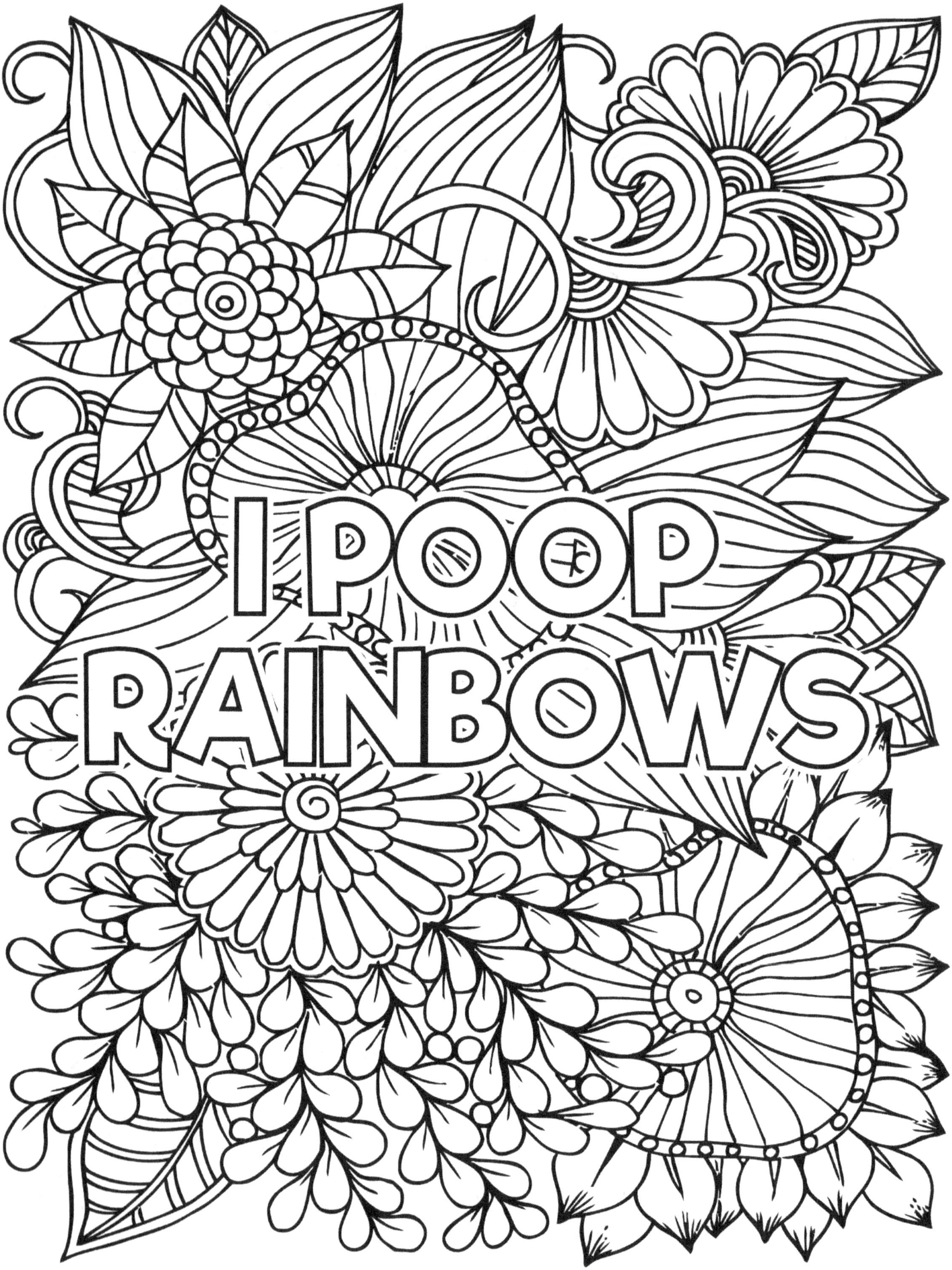
I POOP
RAINBOWS

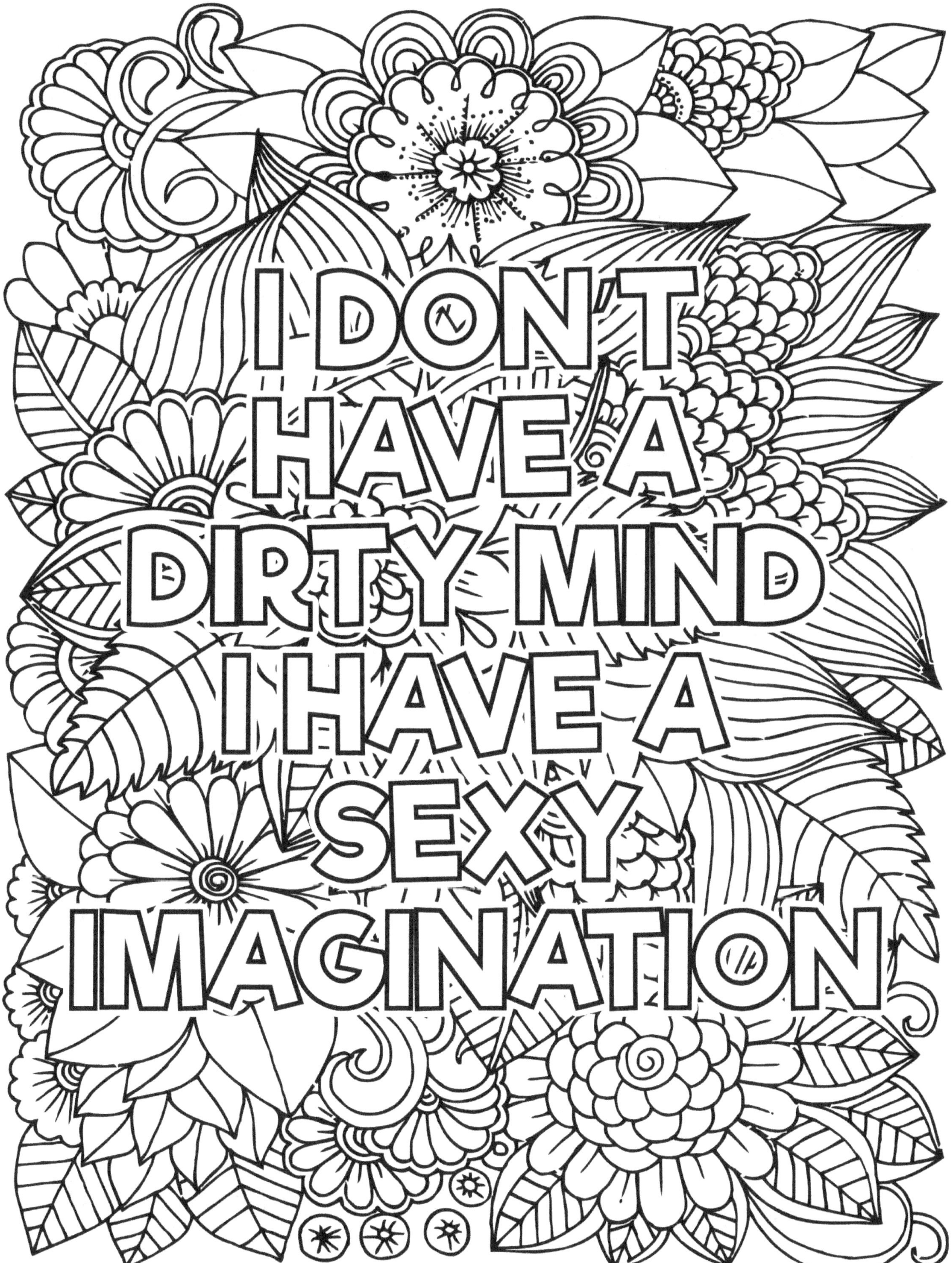
I DON'T
HAVE A
DIRTY MIND
I HAVE A
SEXY
IMAGINATION

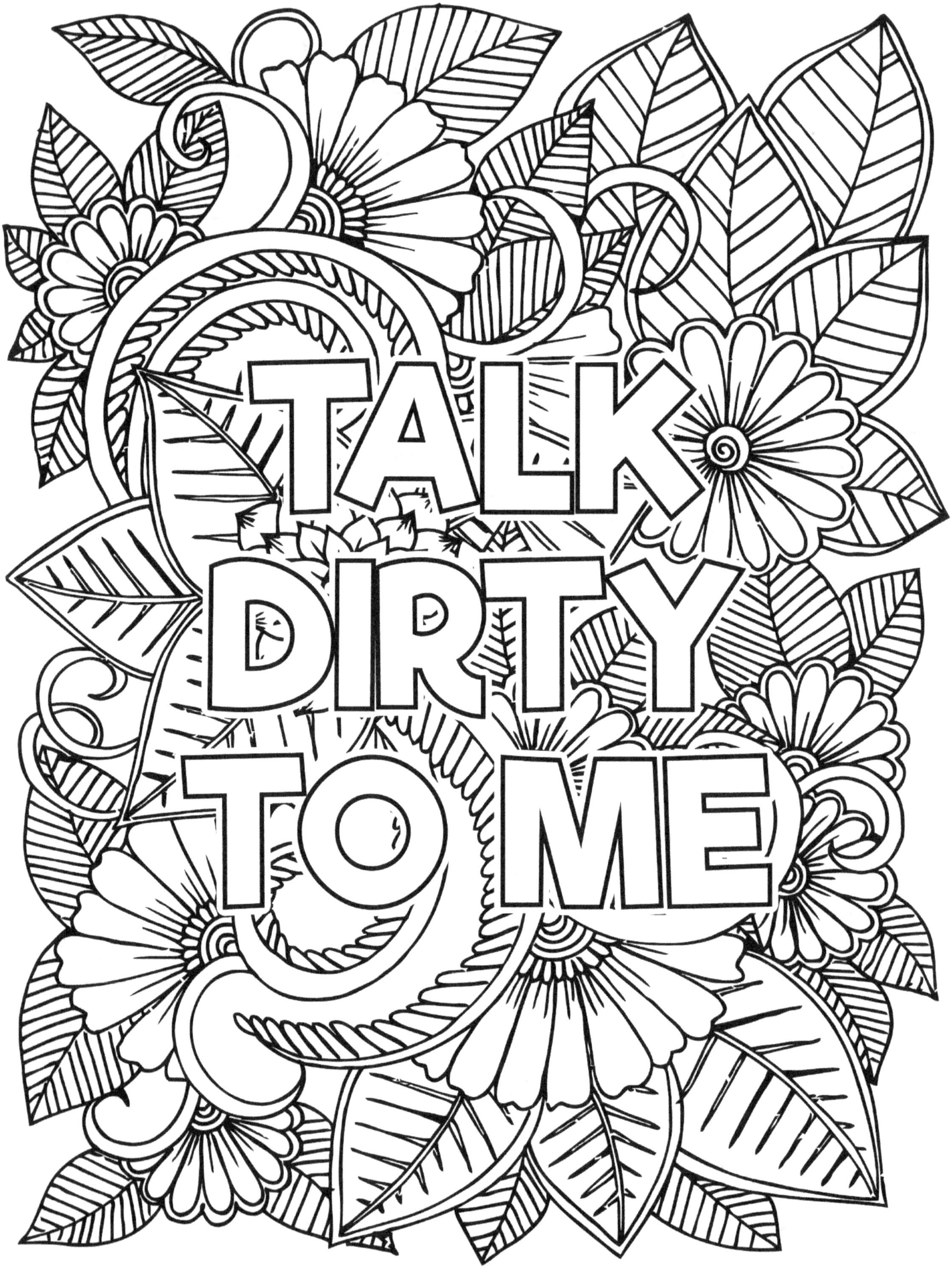
TALK
DIRTY
TO ME

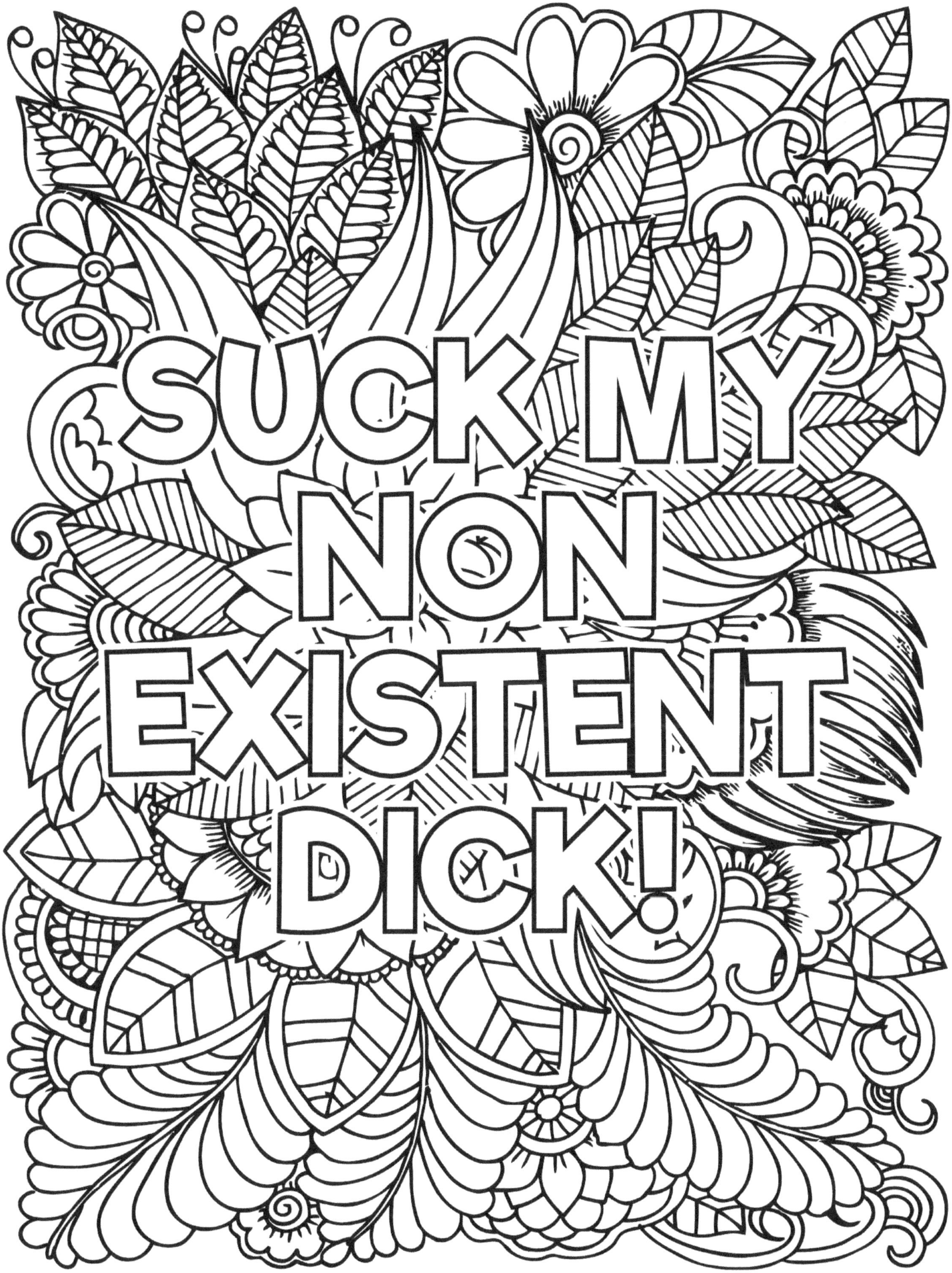
SUCK MY
NON
EXISTENT
DICK!

www.ingramcontent.com/pod-product-compliance
Lightning Source LLC
Chambersburg PA
CBHW080439220526
45465CB00009B/3345
* 9 7 9 8 7 4 4 8 1 9 8 0 4 *